D0983400

The Faust Legend
in Music and Literature

William E. Grim

Studies in the History and Interpretation of Music
Volume 5

The Edwin Mellen Press
Lewiston/Queenston
Lampeter

Library of Congress Cataloging-in-Publication Data

Grim, William E.
  The Faust legend in music and literature.

  (Studies in the history and interpretation of
music ; v. 5)
  Bibliography: p.
  1. Faust, d. ca. 1540—Legends—History and
criticism. 2. Faust, d. ca. 1540—Drama—History and
criticism. 3. Faust, d. ca. 1540—Songs and music—
History and criticism. 4. Music and literature.
I. Title. II. Series.
ML63.G75 1987   780'.08   87-24706
ISBN 0-88946-428-6

This is volume 5 in the continuing series
Studies in the History and Interpretation of Music
Volume 5 ISBN 0-88946-428-6
SHIM Series ISBN 0-88946-426-X

The Edwin Mellen Press   The Edwin Mellen Press
Box 450   Box 67
Lewiston, New York   Queenston, Ontario
USA 14092   L0S 1L0 CANADA

Printed in the United States of America

ML
63
.G75
1988

To Bethany Marie Grim

TABLE OF CONTENTS

*The Faust Legend
in Music and Literature*

INTRODUCTION

It is axiomatic to state that the Faust legend has been the source of much of the greatest literature and music of the past two centuries. A cursory glance at the volumes of Hans Henning's Faust-Bibliographie reveals the enormous creative and scholarly literature that has been engendered by the simple tale of a man who sells his soul to the Devil for power and riches. From its beginnings as a Protestant morality play in the form of Johann Spies' Faustbuch (1587) to more recent incarnations such as Leroy Jenkins' Fresh Faust (a so-called "rap-opera") and the movie Crossroads (concerning an aged man who years ago gave his soul to the Devil in order to discover the secret of performing the blues), the Faust legend has been inextricably linked with music, not only in regard to the many operatic, vocal, and instrumental settings of Faust texts, but also in that Faust and Mephistopheles are very often shown to be musicians. The Devil was traditionally portrayed as a violinist, so it was only logical that Thomas Mann would have his "Faustus," Adrian Leverkühn, be a composer.

In many ways the aesthetic theories of the eighteenth and nineteenth centuries encouraged the linking of music with demonology. Eighteenth-century aestheticians and music theorists, influenced by the philosophy of Immanuel Kant, regarded music as the lowest of the arts because its sensual nature encouraged feeling and intuition over the specific expression of the written word. And when their nineteenth-century counterparts, following the lead of Arthur Schopenhauer, praised music as the loftiest of the arts it was still because of music's emotional appeal, its ability to speak directly to the soul as a direct manifestation of the Will.

It is not surprising, therefore, that Goethe's Faust, caught in the vortex of the intellectual tension between Enlightenment and Romanticism, would prove to be the prime motivator and inspiration for two centuries' worth of musico-literary Fausts. And yet Goethe's Faust, for all of its importance, is a grossly neglected work in spite of the huge dimensions of Faust scholarship. Jane K. Brown has rightfully noted that "It is hard to imagine any writer who has had more impact yet less real influence than Goethe."[1] Brown's statement extends just as easily to Goethe's most famous work, and Faust is a neglected work not because of the limitations of present-day readers to be able to appreciate the work but because of its subject matter. It is perhaps the greatest of ironies in a century which has produced a Stalin and a Hitler that the Devil should not get his due. Modern theology and psychoanalytic theories are in large part to blame for this, because if evil is a treatable mental disease instead of sin, the Devil's usefulness is obviated. When Nietzsche declared God to be dead he also consigned Lucifer to a similar fate, and in the guilt-free society of the twentieth-century West only the most fundamental of evangelical Protestants or the most traditional Roman Catholics and Eastern Orthodox openly acknowledge that the Devil might actually exist.[2] Goethe presciently realized that the Devil is most powerful when he is referred to euphemistically by others:

Witch:
>Sinn und Verstand verlier ich schier,
>Seh ich den Junker Satan wieder hier!

Mephistopheles:
>Den Namen, Weib, verbitt ich mir!

Witch:
>Warum? was hat er Euch getan?

Mephistopheles:
>Er ist schon lang ins Fabelbuch gesch-
>rieben;
>Allein die Menschen sind nichts besser
>dran:
>Den Bösen sind sie los, die Bösen sind
>geblieben.[3]

---

[1] Jane K. Brown, Goethe's Faust: The German Tragedy (Ithaca: Cornell University Press, 1986), p. 32.

[2] It is interesting to note that members of many non-Christian religions have noted the intellectual and religious importance of Goethe's Faust. For a fascinating Buddhist interpretation of Faust see Daisaku Ikeda, "SGI Pres. Ikeda Interprets Faust in Terms of Buddhism" Soka Gakkai News 10:192 (February 1985): 8-15.

[3] Johann Wolfgang von Goethe, Werke (Salzburg: Verlag "Das Bergland-Buch," 1950), p. 812. [Faust, Walter Arndt, translator (New York: W.W. Norton, 1976), p. 61: "Witch: My senses reel with joy and fear/To see young Esquire Satan here! /Meph.: That name's forbidden, hag, you hear?/ Witch: Why of a sudden is it bad?/ Meph.: It's been

The spiritual abyss of the present time may explain in part the neglect of the Faust legend in the twentieth century in spite of the overwhelming activity in this area by literary and musical scholars; however, this is not the point of departure for this book. The emphasis is placed on the musical-literary nexus of several Faust works, on how literary and musical forms mutually inform and influence one another. The first chapter deals with the Faust of Nikolaus Lenau and Franz Liszt's Two Episodes from Lenau's "Faust" (which includes the famous Mephisto Waltz). An examination is made concerning why Liszt was inspired by Lenau's work instead of Goethe's, and any possible points of synaesthesia between the two works will be explored. The next chapter is concerned with Gounod's opera Faust and why that work was and still is so popular in spite of the fact that it is generally regarded as the most unliterary setting of Goethe's Faust (Gounod completely disregarded Part II). The question of whether Gounod's music is in any way representative of Goethe's Faust, and if so, why is this not reflected in the libretto, is examined. The third chapter deals with Boito's opera Mefistofele which probably remains truer to Goethe's Faust than any other operatic setting but has never had the type of popular success of Gounod's Faust. Ferruccio Busoni's opera Doktor Faust is the subject of Chapter IV. In attempting to reinvigorate the musical use of the Faust legend, Busoni based his opera on non-Goethean Faust texts, especially the traditional Puppenspiel. This chapter examines Nietzsche's influence on Busoni, and explores the questions of whether or not the eclectic musical style of Busoni was successful in portraying the ambivalent character of Faust and whether or not Busoni (who acted as his own librettist) was more successful artistically in combining the literary and musical elements in Doktor Faust than in those works produced by collaborative efforts. Finally, the fifth chapter examines Thomas Mann's use of musical metaphors in Doktor Faustus. Mann effectively employed music metaphorically to symbolize the decay of German civilization and the rise to power of the Nazis. Music, disease, and totalitarianism are inextricably linked throughout the novel, and music is portrayed as the

---

consigned to storybooks for youngsters;/ Mind you, men are no better off for that./ The Fiend is gone, the fiends are still amongst us."]

most "Faustian" of the arts. By examining Mann's descriptions in the novel of compositions of Beethoven, Wagner, and other composers, Mann's etiology of musical "sickness" is shown to stem not from the musical radicalism of the twentieth century, but from the beginnings of German music history. The evolution of German music is, for Mann, like the progression of Leverkühn's syphilis and culminates in a fate as strictly determined as that of Faust. Portions of Chapter V appeared in The St. Andrews Review 30 (1986): 125-34 and were read in an expanded version at the 1986 meeting of the German Studies Association under the title of "'An End Without Any Return': Thomas Mann's Description of Beethoven's Op. 111."

The author would like to acknowledge the help and goodwill of the many people who assisted him in the writing of this book. First of all, this book would not have come about had it not been for the enthusiastic encouragement of Dr. Herbert Richardson of the Edwin Mellen Press. It was he who first suggested to me that I write such a book. The patience of my wife Deborah has been extraordinary as has been that of the author's daughter Bethany for whom this book is dedicated. Professor Steven Scher of the Departments of German and Comparative Literature of Dartmouth College has been a friend and mentor in my coming to grips with the myriad complexities of Thomas Mann's Doktor Faustus. I was fortunate to participate in a National Endowment for the Humanities summer seminar on "Literature and Music" that Professor Scher led at Dartmouth during the summer of 1986 where many of the ideas that this book contains received their gestation. Finally, I would like to thank the students who have taken my course on "The Faust Legend in Music and Literature" for their youthful enthusiasm and occasional insights of rare perspicacity.

William E. Grim
Columbus, Ohio
July, 1987

The Faust Legend
in Music and Literature

CHAPTER I

Mephisto Waltz: Franz Liszt
and
Nikolaus Lenau

> Oh, why does loneliness
> exist for us?   Where is
> God?
> --Nikolaus Lenau, Note-
> books--

Nikolaus Franz Niembsch von Strehlenau (1802-1850), better known as Nikolaus Lenau, was one of the most influential poets of the first half of the 19th century, but whose work is almost completely unknown today both in and outside of Europe. That Lenau is remembered is almost entirely due to the fact that much of his poetry was set to music by contemporary composers and that his dramatic works inspired some of the most memorable programmatic instrumental compositions of the romantic era. Of the latter musical category the best known are two compositions of Franz Liszt (1811-1886), the Mephisto Waltz and Der nächtliche Zug (known collectively as Two Episodes from Lenau's "Faust" [1860]), both of which were inspired by Lenau's interpretation of the Faust legend.[1]

Lenau's Faust (1836, revised 1840) was a radically different work from Goethe's immortal drama in both spirit and construction and constitutes a romantic reaction against the enlightened optimism of Goethe. Although it would be pointless to attempt a detailed description of areas of synaesthesia between Lenau's drama and Liszt's music--such attempts are always highly subjective and tendentious--it is, nevertheless, important to examine Lenau's Faust in detail in order to surmise what inspired Liszt to write some of his best known compositions and to determine why Liszt found his inspiration in Lenau instead of Goethe.

---

[1] Liszt also composed a programmatic Faust Symphony (in reality, a set of three tone poems representing Faust, Mephistopheles, and Gretchen), which was undoubtedly inspired by both Lenau and Goethe. Richard Strauss' tone poem Don Juan was inspired by Lenau's poetic work of the same name.

One possible explanation for Liszt's attraction to Lenau is that both men were Hungarian by birth but were culturally removed from their country of origin. Liszt never learned to speak Hungarian fluently and spent the greater part of his life in France, Germany, and Italy, while Lenau was a native of the Banat, a German-speaking enclave in Hungary. Both artists were heavily influenced by Hungarian culture, but this was an exotic feature of their works and was not an intrinsic element. In other words, both Lenau and Liszt could claim a similar ethnic heritage while at the same time maintaining an artistic objectivity resulting from their cultural separation from things Hungarian. Likewise, both men displayed a penchant for wandering in the spiritual as well as the spatial sense. Liszt's perambulations in both areas are well documented and Lenau's are no less far-ranging. Lenau not only travelled throughout Europe but also came to America, the latter experience having a marked influence on the poet and, as will be seen below, being a precipitating factor in the creation of Faust. Lenau's spiritual wandering's were similarly vast. Discussing Lenau's religious beliefs, Hugo Schmidt has remarked that "He [Lenau] was a Catholic who glorified the Reformation and assailed the Pope, a pietist who thought in pantheistic terms, a sensualist who reveled in mystic love imagery."[2]

Liszt's attraction to Lenau's poetry was not only limited to the latter's version of the Faust legend. Liszt set a number of Lenau texts, most notably Der traurige Mönch (1860), one of the most remarkable and unusual compositions of its time. The melody of Der traurige Mönch is based on the whole-tone scale in anticipation of Debussy's impressionistic style, while the text is declaimed instead of sung.[3]

Another possible source of attraction between Liszt and Lenau is the overwhelming sense of Weltschmerz that pervades the poetry of the

---

[2]Hugo Schmidt, "Religious Issues and Images in Lenau's Works" The Germanic Review 39 (1964): 164.

[3]Liszt's anticipation of many of the features of Debussy's impressionistic style is a notable feature of the former's late works. See in particular Liszt's Nuages gris for piano (1885). The declamatory setting of the text of Der traurige Mönch is more in keeping with the style of the then popular melodrama instead of being an "anticipation of Schönberg's Sprechstimme" as suggested by Eleanor Perényi in her book Liszt: The Artist as Romantic Hero (Boston: Little, Brown and Co., 1974), pp. 403-4.

latter; indeed, Lenau has often been referred to as the poet of Weltschmerz par excellence. Liszt, who for all his worldly experiences exhibited noticeable characteristics of world-weariness (as witness his early abandonment of his solo career and his eventual settling in Rome and the taking of minor orders), must have found a psychological affinity with the sense of resignation and aimlessness (even nihilism) that attends much of Lenau's poetry. Liszt was also attracted to the works of other artists associated with Weltschmerz. The most obvious example of this is E.P. Senancour whose novel Obermann inspired Liszt's La vallée d'Obermann from the Swiss year of the Années de pèlerinage (1836).

As a composer Liszt would have been attracted to the musical nature of Lenau's poetry. Lenau not only used music as a motif in much of his poetry (particularly the settings of Hungarian verbunkos, or recruiting dances), but also approximated musical rhythms in his use of poetic meters. Regarding this, Agnes Huszar Vardy has stated:

> Lenau's ability to express in words that which is usually transmitted by music is indeed unique. His treatment reveals an ability to dissolve the dance music in the rhythm of the poem,... while in reality this effect can generally be expressed only through music.[4]

The musical nature of Lenau's poetry is especially evident in Faust, particularly in the well-known scene "The Dance at the Village Inn," one of the two scenes given a musical interpretation by Liszt. Faust and Mephistopheles enter the inn where a dance is taking place. Mephistopheles picks up a violin and begins to play:

Mephistopheles:

Ein wunderlich Geschlecht fürwahr,
Die Brut vom ersten Sünderpaar!
Der mit der Höll' es hat gewagt,
Vor einem Weiblein jetzt verzagt,
Das viel zwar hat an Leibeszierden,
Doch zehnmal mehr noch an Begierden.
    (To the musicians)
Ihr lieben Leutchen euer Bogen

---

[4]Agnes Huszar Vardy, A Study in Austrian Romanticism: Hungarian Influences in Lenau's Poetry (Buffalo, New York: Hungarian Cultural Foundation, 1974), p. 75.

Ist viel zu schläfrig noch gezogen!
Nach eurem Walzer mag sich drehen
Die sieche Lust auf lahmen Zehen,
Doch Jugend nicht voll Blut und Brand.
Reicht eine Geige mir zur Hand,
's wird geben gleich ein andres Klingen,
Und in der Schenk' ein andres Springen![5]

Lenau's decision to make Mephistopheles a violinist serves two purposes: (1) the Devil has traditionally been a violinist and Lenau has continued a tradition that may have its roots in ancient Gypsy lore (i.e., Hungarian) and continues to this very day (as witness Stravinsky's L'Histoire du Soldat); and (2) Lenau gives a contemporary flavor to Faust, inasmuch as the legendary violin virtuoso Niccolo Paganini, who possessed such phenomenal technical prowess, was rumored to be in league with the Devil, and it was Paganini himself who inspired Liszt in his development of a "transcendental" piano technique. Additionally, Lenau was a violinist and, given the autobiographical nature of many of his works, may have imbued the character of Mephistopheles with a few of his own personality traits.[6]

On a more profound and less obvious level, the attraction for Liszt of Lenau's Faust attends largely from its philosophical foundations. Lenau's protagonist is the romantic Faust par excellence; ultimately, he rejects both religion and science. Speaking to Wagner about science, Faust states:

Doch ist die ganze Weisheit nicht genug,
Auch nur den kleinsten Zweifel satt zu speisen.[7]

Later, when a monk reproaches Faust and implores him to return to a righteous existence, Faust replies with a monologue containing this series of rhetorical questions:

Ist diese Welt dadurch entstanden,
Dass Gott sich selber kam abhanden?
Ist Göttliches von Gotte abgefallen,
Um wieder gottwärts heimzuwallen?--

---

[5]Nikolaus Lenau, Sämmtliche Werke (Leipzig: Philipp Reclam, 1883), p. 390.

[6]More than a few scholars have tried to point out similar personality traits between Lenau and Faust (e.g., spiritual doubt, ceaseless wandering, etc.). Given the personal and subjective approach to poetry taken by Lenau, it is not illogical to surmise that similarities between Lenau and Mephistopheles could exist.

[7]Lenau, Sämmtliche Werke, p. 373.

Ist aus urdunkeln Ahnungstiefen,
Worin die Gotteskeime schiefen,
Das Göttliche zuerst erwacht,
Und stieg es auf zur Geistesmacht?
So dass Natur in Hass und Lieben
Als ihre Blüthe Gott getrieben?--
An dieser Frage hängt die Welt,
Doch hab' ich immer sie umsonst gestellt.
Ja! ob die Welt mit ihrem Lauf
Zu nennen ein Hinab? Hinauf?
Ist wohl der ernsten Frage werth;
Wie aber, wenn es ein Hinaus?
Des vollen Gottes Ausstrom, Ueberbraus,
Der nie zurück zu seinem Quelle kehrt?[8]

Having no faith in the eternal verities of either religion or the secular creed of science, Faust, of necessity, seeks absolute authority in his own ego; indeed, Faust is completely submerged in his own ego. And this is precisely the point at which the Fausts of Lenau and Goethe are at their most divergent point. For all of his errors and faulty logic, Goethe's Faust constantly strives for something outside of himself to give purpose and meaning to existence; for Lenau's Faust the search is always internal. The result of this is that the latter is doomed to a solipsistic existence (ending ultimately in suicide), whereas, the former is at least susceptible to the cauterizing influences of outside agents. The possibility of transcendence always remains a viable option for Goethe's Faust, while for Lenau's Faust, in the finite microcosm of his ego, this remains an impossibility to the extent that the transcendent vision could not even be recognized by a mentality so enamored and blinded by its own subjectivity. But Faust, like Lenau and Liszt, lives in an era in which absolutes are as unlikely to be found in personal revelations as in the revealed wisdom of religion and the reproducible proofs of science. After all, was not romanticism an artistic creed which reveled in the incommensurability of phenomena? Nevertheless, Lenau's protagonist continues along the irrational course he has established:

Sag an: was ist der Tod? Was ist das Leben?
Ich find' es nicht; mein Geist will Antwort geben,

---

[8]Ibid., p. 379.

Doch sie ersauft sogleich in meinem Blut....
Den schöpferischen Urgeist zu erkennen,
Mein innerst Wesen ist darauf gestellt,
In meiner ewigen Wurzel mich zu fassen;
Doch ist's verfagt, und Sehnsucht wird zum haffen,
Dass mich die Endlichkeit gefangen hält.
Furchtbarer Zwiespalt ist's und tödtlich bitter,
Wenn innen todt von Fragen ein Gewitter,
Und aussen antwortlose Todtenstille,
Und ein verweigernd ewig starrer Wille.[9]

The irrationality of Faust's behavior is exemplified in the pact scene. Faust agrees to the conditions set forward by Mephistopheles without giving any real consideration as to the efficacy of the powers granted to him in his quest for meaning. The pact, therefore, becomes an event of pure nihilism, lacking the courageous act of will reminiscent of Nietzsche's Übermensch or the desire for transcendence exhibited by Goethe's Faust. Lenau's protagonist in many ways anticipates that quintessential agent of nihilism, namely, Bazarov of Turgenev's Fathers and Sons. Faust's pact (and eventual suicide) is entirely pointless just as Bazarov's contraction of his fatal disease is an exercise in futility. Both characters, having already abandoned religion, eventually abandon science: Faust withdraws from his anatomical laboratory and Bazarov does not even take the modest sanitary precautions to avoid a mortal infection. The sense of irrationality, despair, and egocentrism overwhelms the pact scene from which I quote below at some length:

Mephistopheles:

Verdinge dich mir zum Gesellen
Und hilf mein Waidwerk mir bestellen,
Ich will dafür, bei meinem Leben,
Die Wahrheit dir zum Lohne geben,
Und Ruhm und Ehre, Macht und Gold,
Und Alles was den Sinnen hold.
Von deiner Seel' es sich versteht,
Dass sie mit in den Handel geht.
Lass bluten die verharschte Hand,
Zu schreiben mir das Unterpfand,
Und dass dazu beitrage jeder,
Reich' ich dir diese Hahnenfeder,

---

[9]Ibid., p. 377.

Die ich in einem Forste jüngst,
's war grade Sonntag früh, zu Pfingt,
Dem Raubschütz aus dem Hute zog,
Als ihm in's Herz die Kugel flog.
Recht artlich war es anzuseh'n
Wie so der Dieb, im dichten Laub
Versteckt, auflauscht dem Wildesraub;
Wie doch vier Jäger ihn erspäh'n
Wie er auf sie drei Kugeln sendet,
Von denen jed' ein Leben endet,
Die vierte, ohne Sakrament,
Ihm selber durch die Lungen rennt.
Was ist dir, Faust, du wirst so blass,
Ging dir zu Herzen gar der Spass?

Faust:

So reiche mir den Hahnenkiel:
Doch lass der Laune freches Spiel,
Die widerlich dein Wort mir falzt.
     (Examines the pen)
Der arme Hahn, voll Liebes noth.
Hat selber sich dem bittern Tod,
Und mich der Hölle zugefalzt.
Hier unterschreib' ich den Vertrag
Weil ich nicht länger zweifeln mag.

Mephistopheles:

So recht, mein Faust, es ist gescheh'n:
Leb wohl, auf frohes Wiederseh'n![10]

Lenau's Faust is also ideally suited to musical interpretation because of its formal construction, or more appropriately, its lack of formal construction. Unlike the taut unity of Goethe's drama, Lenau's Faust is episodic in nature, and succeeding scenes do not necessarily elaborate upon previous action. The formal unity of Faust is further attenuated by the additions made by Lenau in the second edition of 1840, particularly the addition of the scene "Das Waldespräch." The episodic nature of Faust lends itself to musical treatment because music must be selective in its approximation of literary material given the lack of specificity inherent in sonic phenomena. Music may have syntax and grammar, but it cannot be said to have prepositional phrases and a vast array of tenses. In other

---

[10]Ibid., pp. 383-84.

words, the symbolic art of music is not easily given over to prosodic treatment.[11] Part of the appeal of <u>Faust</u> for Liszt may have been that its self-contained scenes do not need an elaborate leitmotivic structure à la Wagner in order to convey a sense of musical unity. It is precisely for this reason that all of the attempts to set Goethe's <u>Faust</u> to music have been failures (or severely truncated) to one degree or another. The selectivity necessary for an operatic treatment results in a short-changing of the organic unity of the text, or, as the case of Arrigo Boito's <u>Mefistofele</u> demonstrates,[12] a comprehensive treatment destroys musical unity and comprehensibility. These dual dangers led Ferruccio Busoni to write his own libretto (which is episodic in structure) for his opera <u>Doktor Faust</u>,[13] and we can only regret that Liszt, having apprehended the suitability of Lenau's <u>Faust</u> for musical interpretation, did not see fit to attempt an operatic setting in addition to his instrumental interpretation of two scenes.

The differences between Lenau's and Goethe's interpretations of the Faust legend extend well beyond the domain of formal construction. Lenau began writing his <u>Faust</u> shortly after the publication of Goethe's <u>Faust II</u>, and much of the stimulation for Lenau came from dissatisfaction with the conclusion of <u>Faust II</u>. Although it might seem an act of great temerity to have written a rival Faust so close on the heels of Goethe, Lenau was absolutely correct when he made his famous remark that "Faust is a common property of mankind, not a monopoly of Goethe." Consequently, Lenau's Faust is a very different character from Goethe's Faust, and Lenau may be shown, I believe, to have written a work that is consciously and deliberately anti-Goethean in nature.

The difference between Lenau's and Goethe's conceptions of the character of Faust become apparent very early in both works. In "Night," the initial scene of the main body of <u>Faust I</u>, Goethe has Faust

---

[11]This is true of both literary-based instrumental compositions and operatic works. In <u>Don Quixote</u>, Richard Strauss, of necessity, had to select several episodes from Cervantes' novel for musical treatment. There is simply no way for Strauss to have approximated in music the many pages of elaborate prose descriptions that distinguish <u>Don Quixote</u> or any other novel for that matter. Similarly, the most successful operas, from <u>Il Trovatore</u> to <u>Wozzeck</u>, are episodic in construction.
[12]See Chapter III of this book.
[13]See Chapter IV of this book.

contemplating suicide, but his appreciation for life is restored by the sound of church bells and the choral singing of the Easter service. Faust subsequently replies:

> O tönet fort, ihr süssen Himmelslieder
> Die Träne quillt, die Erde hat mich wieder.[14]

Lenau's Faust, on the other hand, has a completely different reaction to the pealing of church bells. Having climbed a tall mountain to escape the noise of humanity, as soon as Faust hears the church bells he climbs ever higher to escape their sound. Losing his footing, Faust falls and, like Lord Byron's Manfred, is rescued by a hunter, who in this case is actually Mephistopheles. Those who are familiar with Faust I will recognize immediately the vastly different tenor projected by Lenau:

> Nun bleibt er stehn und lauscht dem Glockenklang
> Vom Thal herauf, und fernem Kirchensang;
> Der Glockenruf--die Lieder--mit den Winden
> Dem Ohr des Wandrers schwellen und verschwinden;
> Und wechselnd horcht er auf der Töne Flucht,
> Und spricht hinab in eine tiefe Schlucht:
> "Wie wird mir nun zu Muth mit einem Mal!
> Wie fasst mich plötzlich ungekannte Qual.
> Ich fühl's: des Glaubens letzter Faden reisst,
> Anweht mein Herz ein kalter, finstrer Geist.
> O, dass die Töne, die vom Thal sich schwingen,
> Mich wie ein Aufschrei bitterer Noth durchdringen!
> Da unten Wandrer durch die Wüste zieh'n,
> Und jetzt im Nothgezelt, dem Kirchlein, Knie'n,
> Und die Verlass'nen rufen sehnsuchtsvoll
> Dem Führer, dass er endlich kommen soll.
> Ob eure Sehnsucht betet, fluchet, weint,
> Der Führer nirgends euch erscheint!"--
> Und weiter, höher, steiler treibt die Hast,
> Der unmuth fort der Berge trüben Gast,
> Auf Klippen, wo den Pfad die Furcht verschlingt,
> Wohin verzweifelnd nur die Gemse springt.
> Schon kann der Klang von Thal ihn nicht erreichen;
> Doch fernher tönt's von dumpfen Donnerstreichen
> Zu Füssen jetzt dem ungestümen Frager
> Erbraust ein sturmversammelt Wolkenlager,
> Und wilder stets das Wetter blitzt und kracht;

---

[14]Johann Wolfgang von Goethe, Faust (Weimar: Böhlaus, 1877), lines 783-84. [Translation by Walter Arndt (New York: W.W. Norton, 1976), p. 20, lines 783-84: "Resound, sound on, o sweet celestial chord!/The tear wells up, to Earth I am restored!"]

Er ruft hinab frohlockend in die Nacht:
"Die Wetterwolken hab' ich übersprungen,
Dass sie vergebens mir zu Füssen klaffen,
Nach mir ausstreckend ihre Feuerzungen:
So will ich mich der Geistesnacht entraffen!"
Da plötzlich wankt und weicht von seinem Tritt
Ein Stein und reisst ihn jach zum Abgrund mit;
Doch fasst ihn rettend eine starke Hand
Und stellt ihn ruhig auf den Felsenrand;
Ein finstrer Jäger blickt in's Aug' ihm Stumm,
Und schwindet um das Felseneck hinum.[15]

Lenau's Faust is also very different from Goethe's in that the former truly leads a tragic existence, having lived without purpose or reason to the extent of not even realizing the shallow pleasures of hedonism. In this regard, Goethe's <u>Faust</u> is inaccurately subtitled as a tragedy. His Faust is ultimately rescued from the moral consequences of all of the nefarious deeds he has perpetrated. Lenau's <u>Faust</u>, additionally, never retreats from an oppressive seriousness; there is none of the spirit of badinage or risque banter that permeates the eclectic style of Goethe. This is because Lenau has given the character of Faust a sense of despair infinitely greater than that conceived by Goethe: a despair that is psychological, rather than intellectual, in origin, and as such, is so profound and inescapable as to be all-consuming. Lenau's Faust, lost in his schizophrenic pathos, is the quintessential loner cut off from everything and everybody, and, truly, his behavior strongly resembles that of the anti-social psychopath. Goethe's Faust, conversely, seeks to integrate his existence with that of the universe, and because of this, <u>Faust II</u> is marked by Faust's need for creativity (no matter how ill-conceived or potentially disastrous) that finds expression vicariously in the characters of Homunculus and Euphorion or more directly in attempts to reclaim land from the sea. It is this urge to creativity that Lenau's Faust rejects in every shape and form. Nowhere does Lenau cause his protagonist to engage in a creative act; all of Lenau's actions are negative and destructive. Hugo Schmidt has insightfully remarked that:

---

[15]Lenau, <u>Sämmtliche Werke</u>, pp. 371-72.

> ...[E]xamining the text of Faust without preconceived notions, it will become apparent what attracted Lenau to the subject matter of the Faust legend: not the prospect of theological involvement, but the possibility of showing a character who continuously shifts between spells of deep despair and a display of unlimited power available to him by virtue of his pact. When he cannot resemble God, he turns to the devil who lends him power and induces him to destroy and to kill. Faust and Mephistopheles are cut from the same cloth; they both had aspired to be God. Rejected, they took the diametrically opposite positions and became "countercreators": Faust by abusing his power, Mephistopheles by destroying Faust.[16]

There is a deeper distinction between the Fausts of Lenau and Goethe which has to do with the nature of the search for meaning in life. Goethe's Faust, while preoccupied with discovering a transcendent moment of perfect repose, is in reality searching for his place in the cosmos. Lenau's Faust, in his confusion of dreams with reality, of sleep with wakefulness, has already uncovered a morbid and bizarre temporal transcendence.   It is Faust's laceration, his uprootedness, from both society and place that is partly the result of the self-contained structure of Lenau's scenography and is exemplified in Faust's suicide, an act causing the final separation from both temporality and place.

Just as Lenau's interpretation of the Faust legend appears to be more modern in orientation than Goethe's, so too is it more firmly rooted in the legend's original literary manifestation.   There are a number of significant parallels between Lenau's Faust and the original Faustbuch (1587) of Johann Spies. Most important for this study is the fact that in the Faustbuch Mephistopheles' first appearance is in the guise of the musician.   After conjurations in a magic circle in the middle of a forest, lightning and thunder ensue, and in Spies' words "...whereupon the Devil made him such music of all sorts, as if the Nymphs themselves had been in

---

[16]Schmidt, "Religion," pp. 172-73.

12

[the] place."[17] Like Lenau, Spies has Faust reject both God _and_ science. The pact between Faust and Mephistopheles is very specific in this regard.

> I, Johannes Faustus, doctor, do openly acknowledge with mine own hand, to the greater force and strengthening of this Letter, that siththence I began to study and speculate the course and order of the Elements, I have not found through the gift that is given me from above, any such learning and wisdom, that can bring me to my desires: and for that I find, that men are unable to instruct me any farther in the matter....[18]

Spies' Faust rejects God and science for crass necromancy, while Lenau's Faust rejects both for a pointless and self-destructive nihilism. Another intriguing parallel between the versions of Spies and Lenau arises from the final codicil of the pact in the Faustbuch, namely, that Faust promises not to allow anyone to dissuade him from the course that he has taken. This is extremely important from the Devil's point of view because Christian theology holds out the possibility of salvation, regardless of the degree to which one has transgressed, to the final moment of life. In the final chapter of the Faustbuch, Faust finally begins to feel remorse for his actions and is urged to repent but declines, believing that his sins, like Cain's, are too great even for the forgiveness of God. Lenau's Faust rejects both the spiritual remonstrances of a monk and the secular advice in the form of Spinozan philosophy and the practical homiletics of the character Görg. What Faust has done in both instances is to agree not to be saved from the outset. His adherence to the legal niceties of the pact (which, of course, could have been abrogated at any given moment) has led to suicide: damnation or moral suicide for Spies' Faust and in the case of Lenau's Faust, the actual physical elimination of his human existence.

Aside from the romantic infatuation with modern psychological theories and with the archaisms of the Faustbuch, part of the attraction for Liszt of Lenau's Faust may have been the thin wall of separation between

---

[17] Johann Spies, Faustbuch [1587], translated by P.F., Gentleman [The History of the Damnable Life and Deserved Death of Doctor John Faustus, 1592], spelling and punctuation modernized by William Rose in Paul A. Bates, Faust: Sources, Works, Criticism (New York: Harcourt, Brace & World, Inc., 1969), p. 10. All page numbers refer to the Bates volume.

[18] Ibid., pp. 12-13.

art and autobiography that characterizes the work. This is a phenomenon seen in much of romantic art, namely, that the creative work is a direct manifestation of the artist's innermost feelings, and, by extension, that the greatest works of art are those which express these deeply felt emotions most directly and in which the technical apparatus of art is most subordinated to the immediate, and seemingly subconscious, expression of content (i.e., emotion). By this method, art would almost of necessity tend towards the autobiographical. This is clearly demonstrated in Lenau's Faust, particularly in the many points of convergence in the biographies of the author and his protagonist.

Lenau, like his Faust, was a very restless personality. No one area of scholarship held his interest for long and his university years included study in law, agriculture, chemistry, medicine, and theology, encompassing the four traditional faculties of the university, all of which Faust was supposed to have mastered. Incessant travelling, both in the physical and spiritual senses, was also a hallmark of Lenau's life. No place, no creed, no systematic philosophy could satisfy Lenau's search for spiritual and aesthetic tranquility. Journeying to America in 1832 to escape what he considered to be the moral sterility of Europe and to join the spiritual community established by George Rapp at Economy, Pennsylvania, Lenau quickly became disenchanted with what he perceived to be the even greater moral depravity and rampant materialism of the New World. Seeking solace in nature proved to be of no avail. Ruth Berges describes one of Lenau's sojourns in the American wilderness:

> Once he [Lenau] disappeared for three days. He was found on a high cliff from which he had a breathtaking view. He had not eaten and wanted to die on this spot where he could dream and see better worlds. Having fallen asleep, he thought it cruel to be awakened to a world where he was a stranger and had nothing.[19]

Is this not the same sense of despair Faust holds when he climbs the mountain in order to escape the din of the village below? In a similar physical sense, Faust's sea voyage entails aspects of Lenau's own sea

---

[19]Ruth Berges, "Lenau's Quest in America" The American-German Review 4 (1961-62): p. 16.

voyage to and from America. The ongoing intellectual and theological debates overtly stated and implied in Faust (the critique of Spinoza, the theological influence of Hanns Lassen Martensen, etc.) are similarly those of Lenau.[20]

That aspect of Faust which most closely approximates the realm of music is its preoccupation with dreams. The semiconscious world of dreams was something of a leitmotif for romanticism, an expression of the ineffable and supra-rational. It was music more so than any of the other arts that could engender the transcendence of the dream-like experience. Throughout romanticism, the dream represented a subjective reality, a higher reality as it were, constituting knowledge beyond that capable of being apprehended by the intellect alone. In the Faustbuch, Johann Spies tells of Faust seeing a vision of Hell, being transported up into the air by the

---

[20]For more on this subject see Carl Siegel, "Lenaus Faust und sein Verhältnis zur Philosophie" Kant-Studien 21 (1916): 66-92 and Antal Mádl, "Lenau und die Romantik" Lenau-Forum 2:1-2 (1970): 40-54. The following quotation from the latter article is illustrative of this situation: (pp. 47-48) Lenau-Interpreten sind neuerdings gern bereit, über bestimmte Krisen in Lenaus Schaffen zu sprechen, über die ihn bald der Pantheismus, bald wieder Martensens Anschauungen, dann wieder Hegel hinweghalten. Nimmt man diese Behauptungen für bare Münze, so hätte Lenau nur Krisen erlebt, und es bliebe allein dem jeweiligen Lenauforscher überlassen, ob er bei dem Dichter eine Krise entdeckt, indem er die Wirkung von Spinoza festzustellen glaubt, oder dort, wo Lenau sich von dem "pantheistischen Luder" zu trennen versuchte, usw. Den Anschauungen der einzelnen Literarhistoriker nach kann dementsprechend bald ein katholischer, bald ein pantheistischer oder ein atheistischer Lenau entdeckt werden; oder den verschiedenen Auffassungen gemäss entweder ein Weg festgestellt werden, der vom Pantheismus zu Martensen aufwärts führt und anerkennend gepriesen, der weitere von Martensen zu Hegel als nihilistisch verpönt wird, oder aber das Ganze geschieht umgekehrt.

Die Frage, die Lenaus Faust einmal stellt, "...ob die Welt mit ihrem Lauf/Zu nennen ein Hinab?, Hinauf?" wird auch von seinen Interpreten oft gestellt, ohne sie für Lenau beantworten zu können. Es ist fraglich, ob die Antwort auf alle diese Versuche nicht auch von Lenau selber hergeholt werden sollte? "Wie aber, wenn es ein Hinaus?"--Das heisst, ob nicht alle vorformulierten Thesen endlich einmal beiseite geschoben werden müssten? Ob und wann Lenau eine Krise durchgemacht hat, kann nur auf Grund seiner Werke festgestellt werden; wenn man überhaupt die Frage einfach so formulieren darf, dass man über eine Krise spricht, wo ein gewaltiges, weltanschauliches Ringen zu Werken geführt hat, wie Lenaus Faust, seinem Savonarola, den Albigensern und zum Don-Juan-Fragment. Jede wertvolle dichterische Gestaltung ist ein Ringen, ein Kampf mit dem Stoff, mit der Form, mit der Umwelt und vor allem mit dem eigenen Ich des Dichters. Dieses eigene Ich stand bei Lenau, ähnlich den meisten Romantikern, von Fichte angeregt, stark im Mittelpunkt und rang vor allem mit sich selbst, indem es den eigentlichen Sinn des Lebens suchte. Es ging dabei immer um die Kardinalfrage: liegt der Sinn des Lebens diesseits oder jenseits des Todes, bleibt von diesem Ringen für die Zukunft etwas erhalten oder nicht?

Devil "where he [Faust] had so sweet music that he fell asleep by the way."[21] Lenau's Faust has dreams of similar proportions, however, they are not the result of the Devil's music, but of an unheard music of a terrified and terribly lacerated soul. In the end, after having denied both God and science, Faust doubts his own existence and even his self-inflicted mortal wound seems only a dream:

Faust:

...Ich bin mit Gott fenstinniglich
Verbunden und seit immerdar,
Mit ihm derselbe ganz und gar,
Und Faust ist nicht mein wahres Ich.
Der Faust, der sich mit Forschen trieb,
Und der Teufel sich verschrieb,
Und sein und alles Menschenleben
Des Guten und des Bösen Uebung,
Der Teufel selbst, dem Jener sich ergeben,
Ist nur des Gottesbewusstseins Trübung,
Ein Traum von Gott, ein wirrer Traum,
Des tiefen Meers vergänglich bunter Schaum.
Und zeugt der Mensch, wie Faust, ein Kind,
Ein Traum dem andern sich entspinnt;
In jedem Kind, in jedem Morgenroth
Sich Gottes Phantasie erfrischt.
Und schägt ein Mensch, wie Faust, den andern todt,
Ein Traum dem andern nur verwischt.
Ergreift den Menschensohn mit Macht
Des Forschens Trieb und Ungeduld,
Dass er bei Tag und später Nacht
Um einem Blick der Wahrheit buhlt,
So ist's vielleicht, dass Gott im Traume spürt,
Er träume nur, und dass Erwachensdrang
Im Morgenschlaf an seinem Traume rührt?
Und schlummert er vielleicht nun nimmer lang?--
Du böser Geist, heran! ich spotte dein!
Du Lügengeist! ich lache unferm Bunde,
Den nur der Schein geschloffen mit dem Schein!
Hörst du? wir find getrennt von dieser Stunde!
Zu schwarz und bang, als das ich wesenhaft,
Bin ich ein Traum, entflatternd deiner Haft!
Ich bin ein Traum mit Lust und Schuld und Schmerz,
Und träume mir das Messer in das Herz![22]

[21]Spies, Faustbuch, p. 24.
[22]Lenau, Sämmtliche Werke, p. 454.

CHAPTER II

Faust as Popular Art: Gounod's Faust

> [Er] betrachtet in der Oper die Komponisten als "Wortmörders."--The Countess remarking about the Count in Richard Strauss'Capriccio (1942)--
>
> And of all the dramatic poems in existence Faust is certainly the least suited to be sung integrally from beginning to end.
> --Hector Berlioz, Preface to La Damnation de Faust (1846)

Charles Gounod's opera Faust (1859) is undoubtedly the most problematic musical setting of Goethe's drama and also one of the most popular operas of all time. By 1934 Faust had been performed over 2,000 times throughout the world and the work was the first opera performed at the Metropolitan Opera House on the occasion of its opening on October 22, 1883. For all of its popularity with general audiences, Faust has been reviled as an unliterary perversion of Goethe's Faust, a work so estranged from its original source that it is commonly referred to in German-speaking countries by the title Margarete. Peter Conrad's opinion is typical:

> No romantic opera did justice to [Goethe's] Faust. Gounod makes the philosophical questor languishing and love-sick and turns Mephistopheles into a moustache-twirling dandy with a plume in his cap.[1]

Gounod himself was at a loss to explain the work's popularity, as he remarks in his autobiography:

> Though "Faust" did not strike the public very much at first, it is the greatest theatrical success I have ever had. Do I mean that it is the best thing I have every written? That I cannot tell. I can only reiterate the opinion I have already

---

[1]Peter Conrad, Romantic Opera and Literary Form (Berkeley: University of California Press, 1977), p. 71.

18

expressed, that success is more the result of a certain concatenation of favourable elements and successful conditions, than a proof and criterion of the intrinsic value of a work.[2]

Gounod, unlike Arrigo Boito and Ferruccio Busoni, cannot be held totally responsible for the quality of the libretto of Faust. His librettists, the famous team of Jules Barbier and Michel Carré, never intended to do more than a loose paraphrase (with emendations and additions) of Part I of Goethe's text. Although the nineteenth-century approach to the adaptation of literary works is disconcerting in the present era of philological fastidiousness, it must be noted that Barbier and Carré were well within the established traditions of their day. Patrick J. Smith remarks that:

> The team of Barbier and Carré was most typical of the French opera libretto of the mid-nineteenth century, and the two were in constant demand, both together and singly, for librettos for the major composers, as well as for "boulevard comedies." Their work represents the "number opera" in its standard form in which the polished technique and careful three- or five-act tailoring-- in themselves solid achievements-- were outweighed by the emotional blandness of the situations and characters. Their adaptations of Shakespeare and Goethe have done much to earn them lasting critical enmity, although close inspection reveals that their librettos for Faust, Hamlet, and Roméo et Juliette are only superficially responsive to the originals, and are in truth emotionally tied much more directly to the French operatic tradition of Scribe and, in the case of the Shakespeare restatements, to the popular bowdlerizations still current and exemplified in the works of Jean-François Ducis of the late eighteenth century.[3]

The conception of the opera libretto as literature held by librettists such as Barbier and Carré was, in the terms of Ulrich Weisstein, "Romantic," that is, the view that "the poetry must be altogether the obedient daughter of the music."[4] This view was held not only by artistic hacks but by many of the

[2] Charles Gounod, Autobiographical Reminiscences with Family Letters and Notes on Music, translated by W. Hely Hutchinson (New York: Da Capo Press, 1970), pp. 158-59.

[3] Patrick J. Smith, The Tenth Muse: A Historical Study of the Opera Libretto (New York: Schirmer Books, 1970), pp. 292-93.

[4] Ulrich Weisstein, "Librettology: The Fine Art of Coping with a Chinese Twin" Komparatistische Hefte 5/6 (1982): 24-25. Weisstein enumerates four other conceptions of the opera libretto as literature: (1) the "neo-classical" view, according to which opera is essentially a literary genre; (2) the "Wagnerian" view, according to which opera is a symbiosis of words and music; (3) the "anti-Wagnerian" notion of epic Opera, according to

greatest creative minds of the romantic era.[5] It is understandable, therefore, that Gounod, Barbier, and Carré would subscribe to this view, because their main goal was not, like Boito or Busoni, to advance an artistic or intellectual program, but to score a popular success with the general operatic audience.

Just because Gounod and his associates were following established procedures does not absolve them from the charges that they mutilated one of Western civilization's greatest works of literature. The Faust of Gounod bears only slight resemblance to Goethe's Faust. All of Part II of Goethe's text is eliminated and the only scenes from Part I that are utilized to one degree or another are "Study"; a combination of "Night," "Outside the City Gates," and Auerbach's "Tavern"; "Evening"; "Garden"; "Walpurgis Night"; "Cathedral"; and "Dungeon." The opera is completely given over to the Gretchen tragedy at the expense of Faust's search for meaning in life and the struggle for Faust's soul.

Since Gounod eliminates the "Prologue in Heaven" there is no wager that takes place between Méphistophélès and God. In addition, Faust's despair is for the lack of human companionship instead of intellectual and spiritual unfulfillment and uncertainty. After eschewing

---

which text and music are equal but independent; and (4) the "Baroque" view, according to which opera is primarily spectacle.

[5]Most notable in this regard is Hector Berlioz' famous statement concerning The Damnation of Faust [in Memoirs of Hector Berlioz from 1803 to 1865 comprising his travels in Germany, Italy, Russia, and England, translated by Rachel Holmes and Eleanor Holmes (New York: Dover, 1960)]: "I have already mentioned my writing a march at Vienna, in one night, on the Hungarian air of Rákóczy. The extraordinary effect it produced at Pesth made me resolve to introduce it into Faust, by taking the liberty of placing my hero in Hungary at the opening of the action, and making him present at the march of a Hungarian army across the plain. A German critic considered it most extraordinary in me to have made Faust travel in such a place. I do not see why, and I should not have hesitated in the least to take him anywhere else if it would have benefited my score. I had not bound myself to follow Goethe's plot, and the most eccentric travels may be attributed to such a personage as Faust, without transgressing the bounds of possibility. Other German critics took up the same thesis, and attacked me with even greater violence about my modifications of Goethe's text and plot, just as though there were no other Faust but Goethe's, and as if it were possible to set the whole of such a poem to music without altering its arrangement. I was stupid enough to answer them in the preface to The Damnation of Faust. I have often wondered why these same critics never reproached me about the book of Romeo and Juliet, which is not very like the immortal tragedy. No doubt because Shakespeare was not German. Patriotism! Fetishism! Idiocy!"

gold, glory, and power, Faust tells Méphistophélès what his heart really desires:

> Non! je veux un trésor
> Que les contient tous!-- je veux la jeunesse!
> À moi les plaisirs,
> Les jeunes maîtresses!
> À moi leurs caresses!
> À moi leurs désirs!
> À moi l'énergie
> Des instincts puissants,
> Et la folle orgie
> Du coeur et des sens!
> Ardente jeunesse,
> À moi tes désirs!
> À moi ton ivresse!
> À moi tes plaisirs![6]

Youth and love are all that Faust wants from life. The lofty conception of existence exemplified in the phrase "verweile doch, du bist so schön," the desire for a truly transcendent moment of being, is completely absent. Faust does enjoin Marguerite to linger during their duet, "Il se fait tard,"[7] but the relationship between Gounod's opera and Goethe's drama has become so attenuated that the text of the duet cannot be considered to be any more than the importuning of a desperate lover.

A great deal of the potency of the scene "Night" from Goethe's text is lost in the adaptation for the opera. In the original version, Faust contemplates suicide and is about to take poison from a Communion chalice when he is brought back to his senses by the music of a congregation celebrating Easter. In Gounod's version, a secular chorus of peasants (who are giving thanks for the good harvest) takes the place of the Easter Chorus, thereby losing the effective juxtaposition of Faust's revival with the celebration of the resurrection of Christ and the poignant opposition of literal and figurative manifestations of the Last Supper.

Similarly, the Erdgeist and the microcosm-macrocosm dichotomy are eliminated by Gounod and his librettists. The Erdgeist is unnecessary

---

[6]Jules Barbier and Michel Carré, Faust, Act I: Scene i.

[7]Ibid., "Il se fait tard." ["Marguerite: Il se fait tard, a dieu!/ Faust: Quoi! je t'implore en vain! Attends!/Laisse ta main s'oublier dans la mienne."]

as an intermediary between Faust and Méphistophélès, because Gounod's Faust appeals directly to Satan for assistance.

> Maudites soyez-vous, ô voluptés humaines!
> Maudites soient les chaînes
> Qui me font ramper ici-bas!
> Maudit soit tout ce qui nous leurre,
> Vain espoir qui passe avec l'heure,
> Rêves d'amour ou de combats!
> Maudit soit le bonheur, maudites la science,
> La prière et la foi!
> Maudite sois-tu patience!
> À moi, Satan! à moi.[8]

Gounod and his librettists added material to Goethe's text which is, in many ways, as significant as the deleted sections. Most notable is the added prominence given to the character Siebel (who is little more than a spectator in Goethe's Faust), the youthful defender of Marguerite's virtue and rival of Faust. Siebel is a character of noble intentions but who remains ineffectual throughout the opera. He is a straw man and unworthy opponent who is easily disregarded by Faust. Other additions to the opera include choral sections designed to be crowd-pleasing spectacles, such as the "Song of the Golden Calf" and the "Chorale of the Swords."

Gounod's emphasis on Marguerite is the area in which the opera loses sight of Goethe's drama most completely. The Gretchen tragedy is not the essence of Goethe's Faust, nor was it even a part of the original outline for the drama.[9] It took Goethe many years to solve the problem of tying in the Gretchen tragedy with the conclusion of Part II, and the

---

[8]Ibid., Act I: Scene i. For a further discussion of the significance of the Erdgeist see Chapter III of this volume.

[9]In his estimable Goethe's "Faust": Its Genesis and Purport (Berkely: University of California Press, 1967), Eudo C. Mason states: "...[T]he opening monologue with the invocation of the Erdgeist must at least have been drafted and was pretty certainly also fully worked out, much in the form in which we now know it, before the first scene of the Gretchen tragedy, whichever scene that may have been, was written or even thought of. The Gretchen tragedy is substantially a production of the years 1773-74, and there are no sound grounds for believing that it was begun long before winter 1772-73 at the earliest or that very much remained to be added to it, except the Valentine scene in 1775. There is no hint at all in the entire opening scene that anything like the Gretchen tragedy is to follow, such as Goethe would have been psychologically bound and indeed aesthetically almost obliged to give, if at the time of his writing it the Gretchen tragedy had already been almost completed or even only contemplated." [pp. 188-89]

resolution of this problem was effected only by having Faust become infatuated with Gretchen under the influence of a magic potion. Gounod's Faust is simply love-sick and becomes infatuated with the vision of Marguerite at the spinning wheel:

> À toi, fantôme adorable et charmant!...
> À moi les plaisirs,
> Les jeunes maîtresses!
> À moi leurs caresses!
> À moi leurs désirs![10]

This is in complete contrast to Goethe who wanted to elevate the level of Faust's spiritual and temporal wanderings that occur between the poignant opening and transcendent conclusion of the drama. As Eudo C. Mason has remarked: "...Goethe's Faust says no word about love or happiness, or even about the desire for rejuvenation in the opening scene."[11] Gounod's librettists have also given the tragedy of Marguerite a chronological progression that it did not possess in the original in order to give the libretto a sense of logical plot development. Again, Mason's remarks are particularly appropriate and to the point:

> Altogether, it is impossible to construct anything like a consistent chronological scheme for the Gretchen tragedy, and the later additions, after 1797, make it more impossible than ever: Valentin is killed two days before Walpurgis night, Gretchen is executed immediately after it. All this is quite deliberate and was clearly intended by Goethe from the outset. The order of the scenes is interchangeable: "Wald und Höhle" at first (in the Fragment of 1790) followed upon the actual seduction of Gretchen, but then in 1808 was made to precede it. The "Dom" scene appears in different positions in each of the three texts. All these things would be grave defects, if the play were meant to be on naturalistic or even only on realistic lines, and sometimes they are indeed regarded as defects, for example by Coleridge, who censured Faust I as having "neither causation nor progression." But Goethe has here carefully gone out of his way to avoid the naturalistic and realistic, and was bound to do so, if he did not want the Gretchen theme to ruin his Faust drama completely.[12]

---

[10]Barbier and Carré, Faust, Act I: Scene i.
[11]Mason, Goethe's "Faust", p. 189.
[12]Ibid., p. 204.

But it was precisely Gretchen's humanity, her ability to overshadow dramatically the lofty sentiments and intellectuality of Faust, that was seized upon by Barbier and Carré who knew all too well how to appeal to the sensibilities of the general public. The difference between Marguerite and Faust as characters can be reduced essentially to the difference between being and becoming. The Faust of both Goethe and Gounod is a seeker of something beyond himself; his character is in constant metamorphosis both externally and inwardly. Marguerite, on the other hand, possesses a relatively fixed character in that her role as Faust's dramatic foil or catalyst requires her character to remain constant. The Faust who is first seen brooding in despair in his study is a vastly different Faust from those encountered during the Walpurgis Night, on the Upper Peneios, or ascending to Heaven. The same cannot be said for Gretchen (or Marguerite) whose essential characteristics of naivete and faith are ever present. The immediacy of her character makes her an ideal subject for an opera.[13] Goethe's utilization of the Gretchen episode is in many respects a mockery of the conventions of the operatic stage, in particular the lieto fine. Jane K. Brown sees the inspiration of Gretchen's tragedy in The Beggar's Opera in which the artificiality of opera was openly ridiculed. Concerning Goethe's parodistic intentions in Faust, she states:

> This is, then, still the realm of the "Prelude in the Theatre"; the Gretchen tragedy is precisely the love intrigue described by the clown for the ultimate play within the play (ll.160-165)--

---

[13]The difference between what makes for good operatic characters and literary characters has been noted by several authors of distinction, but perhaps never so clearly as W.H. Auden who was a master librettist as well as a literary giant. In his well-known "Notes on Music and Opera" [in The Dyer's Hand (New York, 1968)] Auden states: "If music in general is an imitation of history, opera in particular is an imitation of human willfulness; it is rooted in the fact that we not only have feelings but insist upon having them at whatever cost to ourselves. Opera, therefore, cannot present character in the novelist's sense of the word, namely, people who are potentially good and bad, active and passive, for music is immediate actuality and neither potentiality nor passivity can live in its presence. This is something a librettist must never forget. Mozart is a greater composer than Rossini but the Figaro of the Marriage is less satisfying, to my mind, than the Figaro of the Barber and the fault, is, I think, Da Ponte's. His Figaro is too interesting a character to be completely translatable into music, so that co-present with the Figaro who is singing, one is conscious of a Figaro who is not singing but thinking to himself. The barber of Seville, on the other hand, who is not a person but a musical busybody, goes into song exactly with nothing over." [p. 470]

> chance meeting, sentiment, involvement, happiness, hindrance, ecstasy, pain-- and its idiom is not, ultimately, that of eighteenth-century tragedy or of Shakespearean tragedy but of opera.[14]

Gounod's Faust, then, is an atavistic work in that the original seriousness of the operatic genre (precisely that which was parodied by Goethe) is returned to in the form of the melodrama of Marguerite's tragedy.

Gounod's characters are not as finely or as deeply drawn as those of Goethe. Mephistopheles is a cynical and suave devil, whereas Méphistophélès appears as an arch-villain. Goethe has Mephistopheles describe himself thusly:

Faust: Nun gut, wer bist du denn?

Meph.: Ein Teil von jener Kraft,

Die stets das Böse will und stets das Gute schafft.

Faust: Was ist mit diesem Rätsel wort gemeint?

Meph.: Ich bin der Geist, der stets verneint!
Und das mit Recht: denn alles, was entsteht,
Ist wert, dass es zugrunde geht;
Drum besser wär's, dass nichts entstünde.
So ist denn alles, was ihr Sünde,
Zerstörung, kurz das Böse nennt,
Mein eigentliches Element.[15]

whereas Gounod's Méhistophélès describes himself as a foppish malefactor:

---

[14]Jane K. Brown, Goethe's Faust: The German Tragedy (Ithaca: Cornell University Press, 1986), p. 114.

[15]Johann Wolfgang von Goethe, Werke (Salzburg: Verlag "Das Bergland-Buch", 1950), pp. 783-84. [Faust, translation by Walter Arndt (New York: W.W. Norton, 1976), p. 33: "Faust: All right-- who are you, then?/ Meph.: Part of the force which would/ Do ever evil, and does ever good./ Faust: And that conundrum of a phrase implies?/ Meph.: The spirit which eternally denies!/ And justly so; for all that which is wrought/ Deserves that it should come to naught;/ Hence it were best if nothing were engendered./ Which is why all things you have rendered/ By terms like sin, destruction-- evil, in brief/ Are my true element-in-chief." (ll. 1334-44)]

Me voici!-- D'où vient ta surprise!
Ne suis-je pas mis à ta guise?
Lépée au côté, la plume au chapeau,
L'escarcelle pleine, un riche manteau
Sur l'épaule;-- en somme
Un vrai gentilhomme![16]

Wagner is portrayed in Gounod's opera as an affable drinking companion but hardly the worthy amanuensis of the learned Doctor. There is nothing to suggest that Wagner could replace Faust as University Rector, as is the case in both Goethe's drama and Ferruccio Busoni's opera Doktor Faust. Curiously, Valentine is probably the one character who is treated in a similar manner by both Goethe and Gounod. Valentine dies defending the honor of his sister who is unworthy of such attention. Realizing the futility of his mortal battle, Valentine forswears his sister and dies honorably.[17]

From a musical standpoint, Gounod does adhere to Goethe's preference for strophic settings of poetic texts; this is seen particularly in Gounod's settings of Goethe's song lyrics. Although Gounod does not employ tonalities in a unifying and consistent manner, he does make use of musical reprises in a very effective manner; for instance, when Marguerite recalls in prison her first meeting with Faust, a short reprise of the waltz music from their initial encounter is given.

---

[16]Barbier and Carré, Faust, Act I: Scene i.

[17]Gounod: [Valentine: Marguerite! Soit maudite!/La mort t'attend sur ton grabat!/ Moi je meurs de ta main/ Et je tombe en soldat!] Goethe: [Valentin: Ich sage, lass die Tränen sein!/ Da du dich sprachst der Ehre los,/ Gabst mir den schwersten Herzensstoss./ Ich gehe durch den Todesschlaf/ Zu Gott ein als Soldat und brav.]

Example 1. Gounod;, Faust, "Prison-Scene" (New York: Kalmus), p. 284.

Somewhat problematic is Gounod's setting of the "Garden" scene ("Seigneur Dieu") in which Faust, Méphistophélès, Marguerite, and Martha appear. It is clear from Goethe's text that the two couples (Faust-Gretchen and Mephistopheles-Marthe) are strolling in a circular pattern and that the couples alternately come into view of the audience. The kaleidoscopic effect produced by Goethe is effaced by Gounod who not only breaks up the constituency of the couples, but also has all four characters singing at once.

Gounod's opera bears very little relationship to other Faust operas in the same way that Monteverdi's L'Orfeo is dissimilar to Gluck's Orfeo ed Euridice. Faust has its origins in the traditions of Scribe and Meyerbeer rather than the highly charged romanticism of Marschner, Weber, Boito, and Busoni. An aesthetic, musical, or textual comparison of Gounod's opera to other musical settings of the Faust legend will ultimately prove to be futile. Too much separates Gounod from the milieu of German romanticism for the comparison to be any more than a matter of personal taste.

There are two lessons to be learned from the above examination of Gounod's Faust. The first is that even the greatest music cannot compensate for a shoddy text. Opera is a hybrid artistic genre and the text must become an integral and organic facet if the genre is to fulfill its artistic potential. Music may or may not be the highest of arts and it is, nevertheless, limited in what it can achieve by itself. As Ulrich Weisstein has stated:

How seriously the quality and unity of opera would be impaired if the verbal rug were to be pulled out from under it is underscored by the limitations in the range of what music can express on its own. Thus it is an open secret that it cannot, or very poorly, duplicate rhetorical devices such as irony, paradox or ambiguity. And while it may, on occasion, be capable of conveying a sense of humor (though not of wit, its intellectual counterpart), it miserably fails when seeking to embody ideas or abstract notions or to show syntactical finesse.[18]

The second and final lesson is that great works of art are great in their totality but not necessarily in their individual components. Gounod would have been wise perhaps to have heeded the words of Friedrich Schlegel who, in discussing the relationship between Faust and Hamlet, remarked:

In reality the coherence of Shakespeare's drama is so simple and lucid that it should be comprehended in its own right by open and unbiased minds. The basis of this coherence, however, often lies so deeply hidden-- the invisible ties, the connections are so delicate-- that even the most ingenious critical analysis will fail if it lacks tact, if false expectations or false principles are applied. In Hamlet all the individual parts develop necessarily from a common center and relate back to it again. Nothing is extraneous, superfluous, or accidental in this masterpiece of artistic wisdom.[19]

---

[18]Weisstein, "Librettology," p. 31.

[19]Emphasis mine. Friedrich Schlegel, ["On Hamlet and Faust as Philosophical Tragedies"] in Johann Wolfgang von Goethe, Faust, translated by Walter Arndt (New York: W.W. Norton 1976), p. 436.

CHAPTER III

Faust Manqué: Boito's Mefistofele

> Boito's Mefistofele is chiefly interesting
> as a proof that a really able literary man
> can turn out a much better opera than
> the average musician can, just as he can
> turn out a much more effective play than
> the average poet.
> --George Bernard Shaw--

Probably the most daring attempt to present Goethe's Faust in musical form was Arrigo Boito's opera Mefistofele (1868; revised 1875). Boito brought considerable credentials to the task: he was a very talented (if overly self-critical) composer, and in his collaborations with Verdi and Ponchielli demonstrated himself to be one of the few opera librettists of unquestioned literary judgment and technique, ranking with such notable figures as Lorenzo da Ponte and Hugo von Hofmannsthal. Boito was also a formidable linguist and was as well aware of the subtleties of Goethe's text as he would later prove to be of Shakespeare's. All told, Boito seemed to be the ideal candidate to set Faust to music.

It was Boito's desire to set both parts of Faust, not just a truncated version of Part I as is the case of Gounod's Faust. This presented almost insurmountable problems of length and scene design which resulted in a disastrous reception for the 6 hour-long original version of Mefistofele when it was premiered at La Scala on March 5, 1868. Boito then began a lengthy process of revision in which half of the opera's original material was excised. Unfortunately, the composer threw away the omitted pages of the original score, so the original scope of the opera can only be estimated. Mefistofele was first performed in its revised version in 1875, was well received, and remains to this day on the fringes of standard operatic repertory.[1]

---

[1]Patrick J. Smith suggests in The Tenth Muse: A Historical Study of the Opera Libretto (New York: Schirmer Books, 1970) that "its [Mefistofele's] next incarnation...was then a success, but his [Boito's] development in the next years into a librettist for

The emphasis upon Mefistofele, as evidenced by the opera's title, is indicative of Boito's membership in the Scapigliato, a loosely-knit group of young Italian intellectuals and artists. The members of the Scapigliato emphasized the darker side of human nature and exhibited a penchant for extreme pessimism. In certain respects the Scapigliato was related to the earlier Weltschmerz movement in Germany and the naturalism evident in the contemporaneous works of the French. It is Boito's fascination with the morbid aspects of Faust's desire for self-fulfillment and with Mefistofele's pandering to the prurient interests of his charge that most clearly distinguish Mefistofele from Goethe's drama. Several generations, after all, do separate Goethe and Boito, and the anomalous features of Mefistofele obtain, for the most part, from the attempt to reconcile within the tenets of romanticism what is essentially an artistic product of the Enlightenment. Goethe's Faust is a man of the mind who seeks active outlets for his creative energy; Boito's Faust, on the other hand, seeks redress of internal emotional conflicts. For Goethe, the operative motivating element of Faust's existence is the search for the transcendent moment; in Mefistofele, Faust is primarily concerned with reconciling the real with the ideal. There is also a considerable difference between the characters of Mephistopheles and Mefistofele. Mephistopheles is a glib and sardonic poseur, a devil-on-the-make whose sophistication blinds him from realizing that he is merely a tool of a higher power. Certainly, there is nothing foreboding in the figure of Mephistopheles whose role is part agent provacateur, part amanuensis, and part ironic commentator. Mefistofele, however, has a split personality. Retained is the witty and urbane devil of the "Prologue in Heaven," (the leader of the loyal opposition one might say), but added to this is a more romantic devil, a conjurer of evil spirits and sulfurous apparitions.

The libretto of Mefistofele, even with its divergences from Goethe and the severe trancations of its extant version, is of a very high literary quality. Boito obviously intended to emphasize the subtle aspects of Goethe's text. In the original version of the opera, even the "Prologue in

---

Ponchielli and Verdi must be regarded, in part, as a critical reaction against the artistic defeat" (p. 334).

the Theatre" is retained. The daring nature of the libretto is revealed by the fact that Boito omitted those sections of Goethe's text that were clearly song lyrics, such as "Gretchen's Spinning Song" and "The Song of the Flea." Whether or not the decision not to set the song lyrics was conscious, it has the effect of concentrating the opera on the struggle between Faust and Mefistofele for Faust's soul instead of diverting the audience's attention to the extraneous story of Margherita. This may explain, in part, why the opera was received so poorly at its premiere. The best known sections of <u>Faust</u>, namely, the song lyrics which had been set so often in the immediate past, were absent. Boito literally forced his audience to confront directly those portions of Goethe's text which are equivocal in nature and sophisticated in construction.

The final version of the libretto is an excellent example of editing and artistic condensation. The salient portions of Goethe's text are presented and connected in a logical manner. The scenography of the opera is as follows:

Prologue in Heaven
Easter Sunday--Pact Scene
The Garden--Faust's Meeting with Margherita
Witches Sabbath
Margherita's Death
Classical Sabbath
Faust's Death

Boito also reduced the myriad personages of <u>Faust</u> to eight principal characters (Mefistofele, Faust, Margherita, Marta, Elena, Wagner, Pantalis, and Nereus) and a variety of choral forces.

What remains of Goethe's drama are highly selective portions of both Parts I and II. These include:

Part I: Prologue in Heaven
Outside the City Gate
Study (after line 1322)
Garden
Walpurgis Night
Dungeon

Part II: Classical Walpurgis Night of Act II
The Helen sections of Act III
Transformed version of Act V

Not only are vast sections of Goethe's text eliminated, but certain sections are expanded or significantly altered. The "Prologue in Heaven," for example, is expanded by approximately 40 lines over Goethe's version. The added lines permit the Cherubim, Penitents, and Celestial Host to engage in a prayer to the Virgin. While not being especially germane to the plot of the opera, this added section is effective as a visual spectacle and provides a counterweight to the increased importance given to Mefistofele.

Particularly important, however, is the manner in which Mefistofele is shaped by the omitted portions of Faust. The absence from the opera of the scene "Night" eliminates Faust's confrontation with the Erdgeist, the latter character meant by Goethe to be an alternative to the conjuration of the Devil by Faust who was too noble a character to do this directly. The Erdgeist's rejection of Faust serves as a motivation for the initial visitation of Mephistopheles who does not appear at Faust's direct request. In the opera there is no motivation for the appearance of Mefistofele save the wager with the Celestial Host. In Boito's case, Faust is the victim of Mefistofele rather than the invoker or inadvertent companion of the Devil. The omission of the Erdgeist clearly gives greater emphasis to Mefistofele at the expense of Faust.

Boito also eliminated all references to the microcosm/macrocosm dichotomy which is given such great emphasis by Goethe in the scenes "Night" and "Study." Goethe has his protagonist contemplate the Sign of the Macrocosmos which causes Faust to question the position and significance of man as microcosmos within the framework of nature (macrocosmos):

> Wie alles sich zum Ganzem webt
> Eins in dem andern wirkt und lebt!
> Wie Himmelskräfte auf- und niedersteigen
> Und sich die goldnen Eimer reichen!
> Mit segenduftenden Schwingen
> Von Himmel durch die Erde dringen,
> Harmonisch all das All durchklingen!
> Welch Schauspiel! Aber ach! ein Schauspiel nur!
> Wo fass ich dich, unendlich Natur?
> Euch Brüste, wo? ihr Quellen alles Lebens,
> An denen Himmel und Erde hängt,

Dahin die welke Brust sich drängt--
Ihr quellt, ihr tränkt, und schmacht ich so vergeben?[2]

If Goethe's Faust is repelled by the thought of human activity being prescribed within the organic relationship of the microcosm to the macrocosm (which motivates the search for a higher existence, ultimately resulting in Faust's reintegration with the totality of the universe), for Boito's Faust this is no concern at all. The psychological despair of Boito's Faust (namely, the attempted reconciliation of the real with the ideal which occurs in the opera's later stages) comes about only after Faust has been provided with a series of experiences via the agency of Mefistofele. Boito's conception of Faust, therefore, is purely romantic and adheres to the romantic aesthetic that life experiences will inform the essentially subjective creative act. By omitting both the microcosm/macrocosm dichotomy and the Erdgeist, Boito has described a Faust initially free of despair and internal conflict. Mefistofele's first appearance finds Faust in an ebullient mood:

Dai campi, dai prati, che innonda
la notte, dai queti sentier
ritorno e di pace,
di calma profonda
son pieno, di sacro mister.
Le torve passioni del core
s'assonnano in placido obblio,
mi ferve soltano l'amore
dell'uomo l'amore di Dio!
Ah! dai campi, dai prati
ritorno e verso l'Evangel
mi sento attratto,
m'accingo a meditar.
Olà. Chi urla?
Il frate? Che vegg'io...
Divider la mia cella io t'acconsento

---

[2]Johann Wolfgang von Goethe, Werke (Salzburg: Verlag "Das Bergland-Buch," 1950), p. 763. [Walter Arndt translator, Faust (New York: W.W. Norton, 1976), p. 12: "How all one common weft contrives,/ Each in the other works and thrives!/ How heavenly forces rising and descending/ Pass golden ewers in exchange unending,/ On wings with blessing fragrant/ From Heaven the earth pervading,/ Fill all the world with harmonies vagrant!/ What glorious show! Yet but a show, alas!/ How, boundless Nature, seize you in my clasp?/ You breasts where, all life's sources twain,/ Both heaven and earth are pressed,/ Where thrusts itself my shriveled breast,/ You brim, you quench, yet I must thirst in vain?" (lines 447-59)]

34

frate, se tu non muggi...
e che?... mi guarda
e non fa motto...
che orribile fantasma
transcinai dietro di me?
Furia, demonio o spettro, sarai mio!
Sulla tua razza è onnipotente il segno di Salomon
(The Friar becomes Mefistofele.)[3]

Compared to the scene "Study" in Faust, Boito has created an almost
festive mood for Mefistofele's first manifestation. From the example above
it is interesting to note that Faust opens a Bible but does not contemplate
its text. This is clearly at odds with the intention and purpose of the Bible
as symbol in Goethe's text. Goethe has Faust translate the beginning of
Genesis, "In the beginning was the Word," into several different versions,
finally settling upon "In the beginning was the Deed." This text, therefore, is
a clarion call to action which functions as Faust's justification for his life of
ceaseless activity. The open but unread Bible in Faust's study in Act I of
Mefistofele, however, presages Faust's eventual contemplation of the Bible
and prayer for salvation in the opera's final scene. Goethe's Faust, then,
literally transcends the word to the deed; Boito's Faust, rather than
progressing, returns to his original point of departure and concludes a task
previously left unfinished.

The full implications of Goethe's text are also mitigated by Boito's
elimination of the "Witch's Kitchen" scene. Goethe solved the problem of
the motivation for the noble Faust's infatuation with Gretchen by making it
the result of the interference of an outside agency, in this case the magic
potion offered by the witch and her retinue of unearthly beasts. In
Mefistofele the motivation for Faust's infatuation is personal desire. Boito's
elimination of much of Part II of Faust logically derives from the elimination

[3]Arrigo Boito, Mefistofele, Act I: Scene ii. ["From the fields and meadows now/
immersed in night, from the quiet paths/ I return, filled with peace,/ profound calm/ and
holy mystery./ My heart's grim passions/ slumber in calm oblivion,/ I am inspired only by
love/ of man, love of God!/ Ah, from the fields and meadows/ I return and to the Gospel/
I feel myself drawn/ and I prepare for meditation./ Ho, there! Who's howling?/ The friar?
What do I see?/ I agree to share my cell with you,/ brother, as long as you don't
bellow.../ what's this?... you stare at me/ but don't say a word.../ What horrible phantom/
have I dragged in behind me?/ Fury, demon or spectre, you shall be mine!/ Over your
brood the sign of Solomon is omnipotent."]

of the "Witch's Kitchen" scene. If Faust's love interest is not the result of magical intercession there is no need to deal with an episode of recuperation from the effects of that intercession, such as Goethe describes in Act I of Part II.

Some of Boito's alterations of Goethe's text may result from the necessities of adhering to the theatrical conventions of the day, catering to Italian taste, and avoiding the censorship that was so common in Italian theatrical productions of the nineteenth century. As a case in point, Faust's salvation scene is significantly altered by Boito. Faust is saved not through the intercession of the "Ewig-Weibliche" nor because of ceaseless striving after unobtainable goals, but because of Faust's prayer for salvation. How very different is Faust's last speech in Mefistofele:

> Dio clemente, m'allontana
> dal demonio mio beffardo,
> non indurmi in tentazione!...
> Santo attimo fuggente,
> arrestati, sei bello!
> A me l'eternità!
> (Faust dies.)[4]

from the analogous section in Goethe's text:

> Nur den verdient sich Freiheit wie das Leben,
> Der täglich sie erobern muss!
> Und so verbringt umrungen von Gefahr,
> Hier Kindheit Mann und Greis sein tüchtig Jahr.
> Solch ein Gewimmel möcht ich sehn!
> Auf freiem Grund mit freiem Volke stehn!
> Zum Augenblicke dürft ich sagen:
> "Verweile doch, du bist so schön!
> Es kann die Spur von meinen Erdetagen
> Nicht in Äonen untergehn."--
> Im Vorgefühl von solchem hohen Glück
> Geniess ich jetzt den höchsten Augenblick.[5]

---

[4]Ibid., "Faust's Death." ["Merciful God, deliver me/ from my mocking demon,/ lead me not into temptation!/... Holy, fleeting moment,/ linger yet, thou art so fair!/ Grant me eternity!.."]

[5]Goethe, p. 1039. [Arndt translation, p. 294: "He only earns both freedom and existence/ Who must reconquer them each day./ And so, ringed all about by perils, here/ Youth, manhood, age will spend their strenuous year./ Such teeming would I see upon this land,/ On acres free among free people stand./ I might entreat the fleeting minute!/ Oh tarry yet, thou art so fair!/ My path on earth, the trace I leave within it/ Eons untold

36

In order to conform more closely with orthodox Christian theology, Boito has Faust's moment of supreme bliss come precisely at the point of spiritual reconciliation; Goethe's Faust, on the other hand, has made no sign of atonement. Salvation is seemingly foreordained because Faust is a being beyond good and evil for whom antinomianism is a matter of course. Both Fausts cause the Devil to lose his wager but for very different reasons. Boito's treatment minimizes the importance of <u>verweile doch, du bist so schön</u> and, by extension, mitigates the necessity and logic of the wager. In <u>Mefistofele</u> the wager is rendered moot by Faust's prayer for salvation. These two treatments of Faust's death also point out a fundamental difference between "Enlightened" and "Romantic" visions of man's purpose in life: for Goethe, Faust's death points toward the ultimate inefficacy of ceaseless striving; for Boito, Faust's death results in the final awareness of that for which struggle is necessary and proper.

Another instance in which Boito may have altered Goethe's text to avoid censorship or controversy is that God does not appear directly; however, the Celestial Host and Mystic Choir appear in His stead. Almost all of the various Italian states of the nineteenth century were very restrictive concerning the literal representation of God and saintly personages on the stage, and this, no doubt, contributed to Boito's treatment of the "Prologue in Heaven."[6]

One of the real achievements of Boito's libretto, even in its attenuated form, is the manner in which both the Gretchen and Helen of

cannot impair./ Foretasting such high happiness to come,/ I savor now my strivings crown and sum. "]

[6]In his very valuable study, <u>Verdi in the Age of Italian Romanticism</u> (New York: Cambridge University Press, 1981), David R.B. Kimbell quotes from regulations brought into effect in 1822 for censors in the Grand Duchy of Tuscany: "Dramas based on subjects taken from the Old Testament are permitted when written by celebrated authors and in a sublime style worthy of the subject, and when the theatre and the means of the impresario provide the necessary facilities for presenting them in a dignified and fitting manner. No performance can be permitted of a drama based on subjects taken from the history and the affairs of the Church" (p. 25). And perhaps more germane to the premiere of <u>Mefistofele</u> at La Scala, Kimbell quotes Torresani, the prefect of police in Milan: "Theatres are designed to correct morals, and must therefore never present anything but moral themes, or, if they present vice and wickedness, it must be done in such a way that virtue appears the more glorious and beautiful as a result" (p. 24).

Troy episodes are combined so as to present a cosmic duality rather than a pair of tawdry love scenes. Boito was able to condense the vast amount of material of <u>Faust Part II</u> into a workable framework for an operatic treatment, and then, in what must be termed as an inspired stroke of genius, he used the condensed material in contrast to, and in expansion of, material taken from Part I. Two problems are solved by this treatment of the text: (1) an organic relationship is established between the two parts of Goethe's text (no mean feat in an opera, a genre which tends to efface the power of literary nuances) and; (2) the seduction of Margherita and her eventual execution are given meaning within the context of the opera. The latter point is especially important because Margherita plays no role in the salvation of Faust as Gretchen does in Goethe's text. Margherita represents the real for Faust, whereas Helen represents the ideal. Faust's struggle, therefore, is not so much against the power of sin and hubris as it is against the duality of human nature. If Faust's baser nature becomes manifest in his relations with Margherita, then his superhuman strivings are reduced to the eponymous figure of Helen. Faust's malady is the romantic "disease" of <u>Zerrissenheit</u>, that is, the conflict arising out of the inability to rectify the real with the ideal. Although this is a fairly subtle point to be made in an opera libretto, it, nevertheless, is stated directly by Faust:

> Ogni mortal
> mister gustai
> il Real, l'Ideale,
> l'amore della vergine,
> l'amore della dea.... Si.
> Ma il Real fu dolore
> e l'Ideal fu sogno.[7]

Boito's conception of Faust is more concretely put forward than the multi-faceted vision of Goethe's, but this should in no way be construed as being either an incomplete portrait or a superceding of Goethe's intentions. Boito and Goethe are alike in that they both recognize the relativity of truth, the constant shifting back and forth between reality and illusion. This does

---

[7] Boito, <u>Mefistofele</u>, "Epilogue." ["Every mortal/ mystery have I savoured,/ The Real, the Ideal,/ the love of a maiden,/ the love of a goddess.... Yes./ But reality brought suffering/ and the Ideal was a dream."]

not mean that there is no truth, but that the search for truth, like Gödel's theorem, always takes the truth-seeker beyond the constraints of recognizable systems whether temporal, material, or moral. Goethe's Faust may be a being beyond good and evil, yet his salvation comes from an inscrutable force, the reasoning of which is beyond the ken of the moral imagination. Likewise, Boito's Faust (whose salvation may be of a more orthodox nature than his predecessor's) is rescued from perdition by a force more sympathetic to the supplicant's stalemate and world-weariness than to the sincerity of his request for salvation.

The elimination of Margherita as a force in Faust's salvation, the minimalizing of the "Ewig-Weibliche," serves to heighten the struggle for Faust's soul as a drama being played out between Faust and Mefistofele. The fact that God only appears indirectly also serves to focus attention to the opera's protagonist and antagonist. It might be reasonably asserted, then, that Mefistofele is Faust's Doppelgänger. Mefistofele presents a grotesque parody of Faust's actions and thoughts in almost every dramatic incident of the opera. In his first appearance with Faust, Mefistofele shows up in the guise of a friar, representing, as it were, a reversal of Faust's desire to attain transcendence via an earthy path.[8] The ruler-servant relationship between Faust and Mefistofele is also reversed at times, particularly in the "Witches Sabbath" scene. As the participants ascend the Brocken Mountains, Mefistofele's power likewise increases. Seated on a throne carved of rock, Mefistofele boldly states:

> Popoli! E scettro e clamide
> non date al Re sovrano?
> La formidabil mano
> vuota dovrô serrar?[9]

Although the substitution of the German Faust (fist) for the Italian mano might have made the pun more obvious, the passage still suggests a

---

[8]In her excellent study, Goethe's Faust: The German Tragedy (Ithaca: Cornell University Press, 1986), Jane K. Brown says of Faust's search for meaning: "repeatedly... the search for transcendent meaning is transformed into the search for meaning within a concrete real world." (pp. 126-27)

[9]Boito, Mefistofele, "Witches Sabbath." ["My people! Why do you not give/ your sovereign king sceptre and royal mantle?/ My formidable fist/ empty must I clench?"]

parody of Faust's lofty ambitions. The opera's final scene also points out a reverse relationship between Faust and Mefistofele. As Faust ascends into Heaven, Mefistofele descends back into Hell. If Faust is unable to reconcile the dual nature of his being as represented by the real and the ideal, then perhaps death is the only means by which the components of this dichotomy can be separated and propelled into their appropriate realms.

The parodistic nature of Mefistofele extends to the musical aspect of the opera as well. When Mefistofele first appears before the Celestial Host, his intoned style of declamation:

Example 1. Boito, <u>Mefistofele</u>, piano reduction by Theodore T. Barker, p. 20,

is a parody of that of the Celestial Host which is obviously supposed to be reminiscent of psalm tone-like recitation:

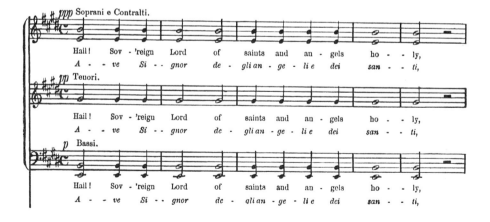

Example 2. Boito, <u>Mefistofele</u>, Barker piano reduction, p. 7

as is that of the Chorus of Cherubim:

Example 3. Boito, <u>Mefistofele</u>, Barker piano reduction, p. 27

Mefistofele also grotesquely parodies Faust's arias. The well-known "Dai campi" in F Major sung by Faust:

Example 4. Boito, <u>Mefistofele</u>, Barker piano reduction, p. 88

reappears, transmogrified into F Minor, when Mefistofele makes his first appearance before Faust:

Example 5. Boito, <u>Mefistofele</u>, Barker piano reduction, p. 94

Even though Boito was forced to make severe cuts in the original version of <u>Mefistofele</u>, a great deal of musical unity is in evidence in the opera's present-day form. This is extremely important because the unifying structure of the music is essential to the realization of the tight organic structure with which Goethe held together the seemingly disparate and disjointed sections of his text. Goethe's unifying procedures are not that apparent on a surface level, but are so skillfully utilized that their true nature becomes manifest only after careful analysis. Harold Jantz states:

> In sum, the unity [of Goethe's <u>Faust</u>] is not a mechanical construct; it stands in analogy to a musical composition, a vast symphony of greatly varied movements and developments presided over by a master in full control who knows where he came from, where he is going to, and exactly and deliberately how he plans to get there. Just as subsequent critical analysis of a large-scale musical composition will even reveal various mathematical symmetries and continuities (which will never be mechanical, which the composer may possibly have arrived at consciously but just as possibly intuitively through a guiding sense of balance), just so the <u>Faust</u> has a more closely knit composition than we may be willing at this stage to attribute to the conscious formal will of its author.[10]

This unifying structure is realized musically by Boito in a number of ways, never more effectively than in his careful and consistent selection of tonalities. Flat keys were generally in those sections of the opera dealing

---

[10]Harold Jantz, "Patterns and Structures in <u>Faust</u>" in <u>Faust</u>, translated by Walter Arndt (New York: W. W. Norton, 1976), p. 553.

with movement, action, and reflection. Sharp keys were reserved for moments of resolution and transcendence:

E Major--   Prologue in Heaven
                         Margherita's Salvation
                         Faust's Salvation
D Major--   Conclusion of the Pact (which
                         parodies the noble nature of
                         the Prologue in Heaven)
G Major--   Conclusion of the Garden Scene
A Major--   Conclusion of the Witches Sabbath

Boito also reprised thematic material for dramatic situations of a similar nature. This is most forcefully demonstrated in the scenes in which Margherita and Faust achieve salvation when thematic material from the "Prologue in Heaven" is restated:

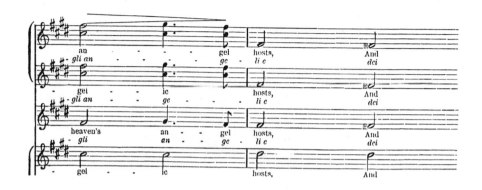

Example 6a. Boito, <u>Mefistofele</u>, "Prologue in
Heaven," Barker piano reduction, p. 48

Example 6b. Boito, <u>Mefistofele</u>, "Margherita's
Salvation, "Barker piano reduction, p. 216

45

Example 6c. Boito, Mefistofele, "Faust's Salvation,"
Barker piano reduction, p. 262

Boito's use of the same musical material for different parts of the text is
very appropriate because it reflects an awareness of Goethe's well-known
aesthetic choice in favor of strophic musical settings instead of through-
composed.

Like Goethe, Boito employed a wide variety of technical devices and
quotations to enhance his score. The following excerpt from the "Witches
Sabbath" is clearly reminiscent of the open 5th harmonies of the beginning
of Liszt's Mephisto Waltz:

46

Example 7. Boito, <u>Mefistofele</u>, Barker piano
reduction, pp. 148-49

Boito was also acutely aware that different styles of vocal declamation were needed for the opera's various characters. In contrast to the cleanly enunciated declamation of the Celestial Host, witness the extremely fast and incomprehensible declamation of the unearthly chorus of the "Witches Sabbath ":

48

Example 8.   Boito, <u>Mefistofele</u>, Barker piano
reduction, pp. 168-69

The reader may assume from the title of this chapter that I judge Mefistofele to be a failure, and indeed, I do regard it as such, but what a glorious failure it is. It is very much a failure in the same way that Henry Adams considered his remarkable career to have been a failure, that is, an impossible task that was not realized to perfection. And in a very real sense, if I may borrow one of Henry Adams' most notable metaphorical utterances, Boito was dealing with a character caught between the flux of the Virgin and the Dynamo, between a higher vision and an ignoble reservoir of raw human energy. The impossibility of reconciling these two forces allowed Faust only one avenue of escape, namely, his own death nominally within the framework of Christian orthodoxy. Faust's dilemma was also Boito's dilemma, and this perhaps engendered a sense of fatalism and pessimism that is evident in the works of the latter. But Boito's "failure" is largely that he anticipated musical and theatrical developments of the next century. Ferruccio Busoni's Doktor Faust is largely unthinkable without the trailblazing influence of Mefistofele[11] in that the latter work serves as a middle ground between the optimistic ambiguity of Goethe and the Nietzschean will-to-power of Busoni.

The reasons for Boito's "failure" have been variously described. Joseph Kerman places the blame on the opera's music:

> Arrigo Boito... was a distinguished literary man and composer with a strong interest in transalpine culture. He was well aware of the stress in later nineteenth-century opera. He had tried to meet it in Mefistofele, the most high-minded Italian opera since the days of Gluck; if he failed, he did so because of his insufficiencies as a composer, not because of any lack of boldness, skill, or understanding of the problem.[12]

---

[11] This is noticed by Patrick J. Smith, who states in The Tenth Muse: "This pessimistic outlook, which has been noted before in the Italian libretto, is reflected in Boito's work, sporadically in the figure of Barnabà and Iago, melodramatically in that of Mefistofele.... This streak of pessimism in the Italian libretto will continue from Boito to the work of another man only half-Italian, Ferruccio Busoni" (pp. 336-37).

[12] Joseph Kerman, Opera as Drama (New York: Vintage Books, 1956), p. 131.

In a review from Boito's time, George Bernard Shaw cited what he thought to be the opera's confusing scenography as the reason for the work's limited success:

> The last act, one of the best sections of the opera, made a marked impression in spite of the late hour; and it is a pity that it is not likely to be secured at an earlier hearing by the omission of the Brocken business, which is musically and scenically childish. So many scenes have already been cut from the original score that the additional injury to the composer's feelings would hardly be felt by him.[13]

But neither Kerman nor Shaw are entirely correct in their appraisals of Mefistofele. Boito attempted so much that Mefistofele was probably a doomed undertaking from the beginning. Even though the composer surmounted many difficulties and created brilliant solutions to the myriad problems posed by his task, the artistic dimensions of Goethe's masterpiece were too great to allow any operatic setting to be more than a mere shadow of the original. When Boito remained true to the artistic ideals of Goethe he failed to satisfy (his) public; when Boito constructed Mefistofele to conform more readily to the artistic conventions of opera he failed to realize in musical form the complete artistic greatness of Faust. Boito's failure, therefore, is that of his protagonist, namely, the age-old inability to reconcile lofty aspirations with a world interested in only the all-too-human. One can imagine Boito agreeing with Faust: "Ma il Real fu dolore/ e l'Ideal fu sogno."[14]

---

[13]George Bernard Shaw, "Boito's Mefistofele," (The Star, 18 July, 1888) in How to Become a Musical Critic (New York: Da Capo Press, 1978), p. 136.

[14]Boito, Mefistofele, "Epilogue." ["But reality brought suffering/ and the Ideal was a dream."]

CHAPTER IV

Faust as Magician: Busoni's <u>Doktor Faust</u>

> That which does not destroy me makes me stronger.
>
> --Friedrich Nietzsche--

Ferruccio Busoni's operatic masterpiece <u>Doktor Faust</u> (1924) was the culmination of a lifetime of musical experimentation and philosophical speculation. The composition of <u>Doktor Faust</u> occupied the last 15 years of the composer's life and, like Berg's <u>Lulu</u>, was fully complete at the time of Busoni's death except for the final scene which was realized by the composer's protegé Philipp Jarnach. Originally begun as an opera about Leonardo da Vinci, the "Italian Faust," Busoni then abandoned his plans and contemplated Merlin as a subject before settling upon Faust as protagonist. Although Busoni eschewed most of the musical features of the Wagnerian music drama, his method of composition did approach that of Wagner's in that Busoni was his own librettist and completed the libretto of <u>Doktor Faust</u> many years before the music was completed.

The opera exhibits a highly original harmonic vocabulary and philosophical approach to the Faust legend as well as a truly revitalized approach to its dramatic presentation. <u>Doktor Faust</u> anticipates many of the most advanced features of the operas of Berg, Britten, and Stravinsky, particularly the psychological portrayal of its characters, the ambivalent relationship between Faust and Mephistopheles, and the reestablishment of the chorus to a position of intrinsic importance.

Busoni was a dedicated and knowledgeable student of Goethe and was well aware of the almost impossible task of rendering the entirety of <u>Faust</u> into a comprehensible and performable opera. As a young man Busoni had befriended Arrigo Boito and was present at both the rehearsals and performances of the latter's <u>Mefistofele</u> in Arezzo in 1882[1] and, therefore, was well aware of the great difficulties that Boito had encountered in the production of his opera and the several severe revisions that were necessary before <u>Mefistofele</u> gained critical and popular success. As a result, Busoni decided to base his opera upon the traditional <u>Puppenspiel</u> instead of Goethe's drama. This choice immediately solved the problems of the opera's duration and the obvious comparisons that would be made between the opera and Goethe's <u>Faust</u>, which presumably would have been to the detriment of the former. Although Busoni went further back in time than Goethe for the basis of his opera, there are unmistakable traces of Goethe's influence in <u>Doktor Faust</u>, particularly in Faust's attainment of self-awareness, which in this case results in a personal transcendence of the ego through the sheer effort of the will instead of the intercession of the "<u>Ewig-Weibliche</u>."

The musical structure of <u>Doktor Faust</u> consciously avoids the characteristics of the Wagnerian music drama. Indeed, Busoni viewed Wagner as representing a dead-end for later generations of composers. In "A Sketch of a New Esthetic of Music," Busoni stated:

> Wagner, a Germanic Titan, who touched our earthly horizon in orchestral tone-effect, who intensified the form of expression, but fashioned it into a <u>system</u> (music-drama, declamation, leading-motive), is on this account incapable of further intensification. His category begins and ends with himself; first, because his self-imposed task was of such a nature, that it could be achieved by one man alone.[2]

Leitmotivic structure is not utilized in <u>Doktor Faust</u>; indeed, at a first listening, the opera gives the impression of being through-composed. Repetitive musical motives do occur, but there is no consistency in the manner in which they are allied with the text. As an example, one of the most common melodic motifs in the opera contains the interval of the major sixth followed by the raising and lowering of a semitone. One

---

[1] Ferruccio Busoni, <u>The Essence of Music and Other Papers</u>, translated by Raymond Ley (New York: Philosophical Library, 1957), pp. 167-70.
[2] Ferruccio Busoni, "A Sketch of a New Esthetic of Music" in <u>Three Classics in the Aesthetic of Music</u>, translated by Th. Baker (New York: Dover Publications, 1962), p. 80.

instance of this occurs at the first appearance of the three students from Crakow in Vorspiel I:

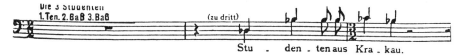

Example 1. Busoni, <u>Doktor Faust</u>, Vorspiel I (after Rehearsal No. 32) [p. 23 of piano score by Egon Petri and Michael von Zadora].

Another of the many occurrences of this motif appears in the first scene of the main play with the action taking place in the ducal palace at Parma:

Example 2. Busoni, <u>Doktor Faust</u>, Hauptspiel, Bild 1 (at Rehearsal No. 38) [pp. 155 of the Petri-von Zadora piano score].

Clearly there is no textual relationship between the two occurrences of the motif. Another related example is Busoni's decision not to use in a consistent manner the obvious literary symbolism inherent in the interval of the tritone (the "diabolus in musica"). The tritone is outlined in the first mention of the magical book presented to Faust by the three students from Crakow:

54

Example 3a. Busoni, <u>Doktor Faust</u>, Vorspiel I (after Rehearsal No. 23) [pp. 17-18 of the Petri-von Zadora piano score].

appears again as Faust bids Lucifer to appear:

Example 3b. Busoni, <u>Doktor Faust</u>, Vorspiel II (after Rehearsal No. 9) [p. 36 of the Petri-von Zadora piano score].

and is used as an invocation of Faust's presence:

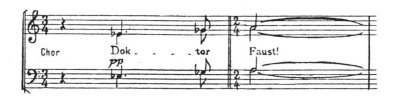

Example 3c. Busoni, <u>Doktor Faust</u>, Hauptspiel, Bild 1 (after Rehearsal No. 25) [p. 148 of the Petri-von Zadora piano score].

Busoni also uses the ambivalent harmonic sense of the tritone as the background for interrogatory settings such as this:

Example 3d. Busoni, <u>Doktor Faust</u>, Vorspiel II (after Rehearsal No. 57) [p. 67 of the Petri-von Zadora piano score].

And finally, the tritone is featured prominently in the "debate" between the opposing choruses of Protestant and Catholic students in the opera's tavern scene:[3]

---

[3]Although Busoni had a critical opinion of the church, saying at one point that he desired to move beyond both "Wagner and Christianity," it is apparent that his use of the tritone at this particular point is not meant to be parodistic in nature, but as an active melodic interval motivating the ensuing double choral section.

56

Example 3e. Busoni, Doktor Faust, Hauptspiel, Bild 3 (Rehearsal No. 24)
[p. 215 of the Petri-von Zadora piano score].

Busoni is employing musical motifs strictly for their functioning within musical contexts and not for any extra-musical purposes. The music "fits" the words in that it evokes an appropriate psychological background for the declamation of the text without implying more than an impressionistic relationship between the music and the text. This goes along precisely with Busoni's aesthetic of opera, to wit, that the conventions of opera (i.e., musical and literary forms) should be evident to the audience, that the audience should be "in" on the imaginary world created by the composer. In his essay, "The Score of Doktor Faust," Busoni states that: "The principal thing for me was to mould musically independent forms which at the same time suited the words and the scenic events and which also had a separate and sensible existence detached from the words and the situation."[4]

Implicit in Busoni's separation of music and text into separate spheres of development is the idea that in opera music serves as a metaphor, instead of a direct representation, of the dramatic action and

[4]Ferruccio Busoni, "The Score of Doktor Faust" in The Essence of Music and Other Papers, translated by Rosamund Ley (New York: Philosophical Library, 1957), p. 73.

character development. In other words, the organic development of the music serves as a symbol for the organic development of the plot and of the characters themselves. The concept of organicism provides to a great extent a rationale for the musical procedures and literary techniques employed by Busoni in <u>Doktor Faust</u>. The rejection of the Wagnerian leitmotif stems from Busoni's belief in the underlying organic nature of musical forms. Speaking of the motive in particular, Busoni remarks:

> Every motive--so it seems to me--contains, like a seed, its life-germ within itself. From the different plant-seeds grow different families of plants, dissimilar in form, foliage, blossom, fruit, growth and color.
> Even each individual plant belonging to one and the same species assumes, in size, form and strength, a growth peculiar to itself. And so, in each motive, there lies the embryo of its fully developed form; each one must unfold itself differently, yet each obediently follows the law of eternal harmony. <u>This form is imperishable, though each be unlike every other</u>.
> The motive in a composition with program bears within itself the same natural necessity; but it must, even in its earliest phase of development, renounce <u>its own proper mode of growth</u> to mould--or, rather, twist--itself to fit the needs of the program. Thus turned aside, at the outset, from the path traced by nature, it finally arrives at a wholly unexpected climax, whither it has been led, not by its own organization, but by the way laid down in the program, or the action, or the philosophical idea.
> And how primitive must this art remain! True, there are unequivocal descriptive effects of tone-painting (from these the entire principle took its rise), but these means of expression are few and trivial, covering a very small section of musical art.[5]

Busoni's organicism clearly precludes the recurring representational force of the leitmotif and rejects the crass <u>mimesis</u> of extra-musical events; however, by allowing the music of <u>Doktor Faust</u> to develop in a purely musical manner, Busoni has cunningly changed the role of music from direct representation of the text to that of a biological analogy for the character development of the protagonist. Busoni was not alone in his preoccupation with organicism. In a way, organicism was a late romantic

---

[5]Busoni, "Sketch," p. 81.

manifestation of pantheism: instead of seeing God in every aspect of nature, the organicist views nature as being subject to forces (or even natural laws in the 18th-century sense) which are of an immutable nature. All objects, by this line of reasoning, are subject to a process of historicism in the sense suggested by Karl Popper.[6] What distinguishes the late 19th century-early 20th century organicist from the 18th-century seeker of natural laws to explain artistic phenomena is the former's unwillingness to accede to the latter's confidence in discerning the course of organic and evolutionary processes.[7]

Busoni's method, therefore, poses one very significant ontological difficulty: his faith in the "natural" development of organic musical forms (which presupposes artistic objectivity and implies a mechanically deterministic approach to musical composition) is seemingly at odds with his acknowledgement of the prerogative of the creative artist to break established rules of artistic procedure.[8] The clue to the solution of this dilemma is mentioned in passing in the "Sketch of a New Esthetic of Music": "[The creator]...should seek out and formulate a fitting individual law, which, after the first complete realization, he should annul, that he himself may not be drawn into repetitions when his next work shall be in the making."[9] In other words, Busoni suggests that the creative artist boldly breaks away from what he has done in the past in the faith that his artistic intuition will somehow apprehend the next stage in his creative development.

Busoni's approach to artistic creativity as evidenced in <u>Doktor Faust</u> posits a dichotomy between intellect and instinct and closely resembles the

---

[6]See the particular Karl Popper, <u>The Poverty of Historicism</u> (Boston, 1957).

[7]This is not to say that musical organicists have not attempted to create and elaborate upon "laws" of musical evolution and development, but that their efforts have largely been shown to be subjective and "unscientific" in nature. A very substantial critical literature of musical organicism and the "natural laws" of music exists by theorists including Jean-Phillipe Rameau, Heinrich Schenker, Rudolf Reti, and Paul Hindemith.

[8]The "Sketch of a New Esthetic of Music" is replete with passages stressing this need. For example, "The creator should take over no traditional law in blind belief, which would make him view his own creative endeavor, from the outset, as an exception contrasting with the law..." and "The function of the creative artist consists in making laws, not in following laws ready made. He who follows such laws, ceases to be a creator" (p. 88).

[9]<u>Ibid.</u>, p. 88.

bifurcation of human intelligence as proposed by Henri Bergson. In Creative Evolution, Bergson states:

> While intelligence treats everything mechanically, instinct proceeds, so to speak, organically.... The most essential of the primary instincts are really, therefore, vital processes. The potential consciousness that accompanies them is generally actualized only at the outset of the act, and leaves the rest of the process to go on by itself.[10]

The intellect, while capable of classifying ideas and objects into systems of representational or symbolic thought, is incapable of initiating creative or evolutionary processes.[11] Creativity, then, proceeds from an ironic basis: the conscious and intelligible courage to place faith in the generative powers of instinct, or, in other words, the will to venture forth into the unchart ed realm of human existence. Bergson states further that:

> When we put back our being into our will, and our will itself into the impulsion it prolongs, we understand, we feel, that reality is a perpetual growth, a creation pursued without end. Our will already performs this miracle. Every human work in which there is invention, every voluntary act in which there is freedom, every movement of an organism that manifests spontaneity, brings something new into the world.[12]

It is no wonder, then, that Busoni was strongly attracted to the Faust legend, especially Faust's constant quest for a higher level of intellectual existence, and ultimately, a higher state of self-awareness. Doktor Faust, therefore, consists of evolutionary thought on three levels. Busoni's evolution as a composer is represented by the organic development of his compositional processes which, in turn, provides an analogy to the personal evolution and dramatic development of Faust. And Busoni's Faust, more so than any previous manifestation of the legend, exhibits the spontaneity of action that Bergson characterizes as the vital component of creative evolution. Faust is not a character given to hesitation. In Vorspiel

---

[10]Henri Bergson, Creative Evolution, authorized translation by Arthur Mitchell (New York: Random House [The Modern Library], 1944), p. 182.

[11]Ibid., p. 173. ["Suffice it to say that the intellect is characterized by the unlimited power of decomposing according to any law or of recomposing into any system."]

[12]Ibid., p. 261.

I, Faust tells Wagner to dismiss the three visitors who have come to his home, and upon learning that they are from Crakow, just as abruptly invites them in. Likewise, in Vorspiel II, Faust does not hesitate to request Mephistopheles to eliminate his enemies through murderous intercession:

> Meph. Kommt es einmal zum Letzten,
> dann find meinesgleichen,
> dann bin ich geringerer Teufel
> als Retter gefällig zur Stelle,
> höre Faust: Ich gebe dir Reichtum und
> Macht, freunden der Liebe, weitesten
> Ruhmesglanz, weltlichen Ruhm. Offen
> find dir die herrlichkeiten dieser Erde.
>
> Faust. Ende!
>
> Meph. So stehn die Dinge. Wähle!
>
> Faust. Schlau wusstest du die Schlingen zu
> legen.
>
> Meph. Schlag' ein.
>
> Faust. Niemals!
>
> Meph. Deine Schergen stehn dahinter. Ein
> Wort von dir, und sie find nicht mehr!
>
> Faust. Töte sie.
>
> Meph. Es ist geschehn.[13]

The impulsive nature of Faust is strengthened by the dramatic structure of the opera. The conscious omission of superfluous material increases the dramatic flow, a lesson no doubt learned from Boito's difficulties with Mefistofele. In fact, many of the most memorable scenes of Goethe's Faust either occur offstage or are only implied in Doktor Faust. The overall dramatic structure is as follows:

---

[13]Ferruccio Busoni, Doktor Faust: Dichtung und Musik (Wiesbaden: Breitkopf & Härtel, 1925/53), pp. 14-15.

Symphonia	Prologue to the Audience
Vorspiel I	Wittenberg: Faust's Study
Vorspiel II	Faust's Study at Midnight (the same day)
Interlude	A Romanesque Chapel
Hauptspiel: Scene 1	The Ducal Court at Parma
Symphonic Intermezzo	Sarabande
Scene 2	A Tavern in Wittenberg
Scene 3	A Snow-Covered Street in Wittenberg

The action is tightly condensed. After an opening prologue in which Busoni's operatic philosophy is recited in verse the events of the opera move rather quickly. Faust is first seen in his study and is visited by three students from Crakow who present him with a book of magic, a key, and a deed assigning ownership of the items. Faust then invokes the Devil who appears in six manifestations, the final being Mephistopheles. After Faust requests Mephistopheles' assistance in disposing of his creditors and pursuers, the pact is signed to the ironic accompaniment of the Easter chorus. Valentine, the brother of the girl Faust has seduced (in the opera she neither appears nor is named), is killed in church and the Hauptspiel is about to begin. Faust and Mephistopheles intrude upon the wedding festivities of the Duke of Parma. After conjuring up the images of the Queen of Sheba, Samson and Delilah, and John the Baptist and Salome, Faust runs off with the Duchess before the wedding is complete. Mephistopheles advises the Duke to marry the sister of the Duke of Ferrara instead for matters of state security. The scene then shifts to the tavern in Wittenberg in which rival groups of Protestant and Catholic students are holding forth in an intellectual debate. Faust thinks wistfully of the Duchess whom he has abandoned. Mephistopheles arrives and announces that the Duchess is dead and that Faust has fathered a child with the Duchess. Mephistopheles drops the dead body of a child before Faust; however,

Mephistopheles transforms the dead body into straw which is then burned and transformed into a vision of Helen of Troy. The vision of Helen vanishes as Faust attempts to embrace it. The three students from Crakow return and demand their magical gifts back, but Faust is unable to do so because he has lost them. The three students leave but not before prophesizing Faust's death at midnight. In the final scene Wagner has been named Rector of the University and now resides in Faust's former house. Faust sees a beggar woman who turns out to be the Duchess. She gives Faust their dead child and tells him that there is still time to complete his task. Kneeling before a cross, Faust is unable to remember the words to any prayers. He puts the child on the ground and makes a magic circle. In his last living act, Faust transfers his will to the child who rises up and moves away into town. Mephistopheles, in the guise of the night watchman, sees Faust's dead body and asks rhetorically, "Sollte dieser Mann verunglückt sein?"

Busoni's sparse approach to the dramatic structure of the opera offers several interesting new dimensions. Faust's seduction of the Gretchen character takes place before the opera even begins. This gives more importance to the love interest between Faust and the Duchess of Parma (and vicariously to Helen of Troy). For all of Busoni's remonstrances against the operatic convention of the love-duet, he was not averse to having his protagonist display considerable infatuation with a female character. The greater emphasis given to the Duchess at the complete neglect of the Gretchen character does not infer a complete renunciation of the concept of "das Ewig-Weibliche," but an insistence that love should transcend sentimentality, and in so doing, Busoni has given Faust a love interest worthy of his station and lofty intellectual nature.[14]

The actual signing of Faust's pact with the Devil is, for all intents and purposes, an anti-climactic event. The signing of the pact does not bring into being a new chain of sinful activities or cause a change in Faust's status, but is rather the logical conclusion of a set of four actions initiated

---

[14]Friedrich Nietzsche's main complaint against Goethe's <u>Faust</u> was that he did not believe that a character of Faust's nature would trifle with such an insignificant woman as Gretchen.

by Faust himself, each of which could be considered as a pact with the Devil. First of all, Faust's seduction of the woman (as already mentioned) and the incurring of debts and other crimes are committed before the opera begins. Secondly, Faust accepts the magic book, key, and title deed (a type of pact implying ownership) from the three students from Crakow. Thirdly, Faust invokes the presence of the Devil and dismisses five manifestations before settling on Mephistopheles. Finally, Faust requests Mephistopheles to kill his enemies before the signing of the pact and Mephistopheles agrees to do so. Each of these four actions implies a pact with the Devil (either of an oral or written variety) before the actual legalistic signing of the document. Busoni has taken great pains to demonstrate that the pact is not an active measure of sympathetic magic but is the result of Faust's will. Unlike the signing of a property deed, Faust's signature does not bring about a new contractual relationship because Faust's relationship with the Devil is a proprietary one and predates the convenant signed in blood.

Faust's relationship vis-à-vis Mephistopheles undergoes a similar evolutionary transformation. At first, Mephistopheles assumes a role as Faust's superior, particularly after the latter has stepped out of the security of the magic circle. Mephistopheles will grant Faust the fulfillment of his desires but only at the price of the latter's eventual servitude to the former:

> Faust. Beschaffe mir für meines
> Lebens Rest
> die unbedingte Erfüllung jeden Wunsches,
> lass mich die Welt umfassen,
> --den Osten und den Süden, die mich
> rufen--
> lass mich des Menschen Tun vollauf
> begreifen
> und ungeahnt erweitern;
> gib mir Genie,
> und gib mir auch sein Leiden,
> auf dass ich glücklich werde wie kein
> andrer.
>
> Meph. Weiter, nur weiter, falls Ich etwa
> nicht zu Ende wär't.

64

Faust. O, lass mich die Welt umfassen,
       der Menschen Tun begreifen,
       es ungeahnt erweitern; gib mir Genie,
       gib mir auch sein Leiden.

Meph. Was noch mehr?

Faust. Mache mich frei!
       so dientest du mir recht, bis an die
       Erschöpfung, hernach--
       Jetzt fordre du.

Meph. Hernach dienest du mir, fortab.[15]

In the Hauptspiel, Mephistopheles serves as Faust's amanuensis and advisor, appearing in Scene 1 as the herald of Faust's entrance into the ducal court and warning Faust about the possibility that the food of the wedding feast is poisoned. In Scene 2, Mephistopheles appears at the Tavern and announces that the Duchess is dead and presents Faust with the dead child he has fathered. The logic of this particular incident is somewhat curious except when viewed in relation to both the action which has already occurred and to the conclusion of the opera. Mephistopheles does not act in a direct manner at any time during the opera; his main function is as a catalyst or <u>agent provacateur</u>. He convinces (rather than forces) the soldiers to kill Valentine; it is Faust, not Mephistopheles, who conjures up the images of historical personages at the wedding. And at the Tavern, Mephistopheles' announcement that the Duchess is dead is a lie (she reappears in Scene 3), and the dead body of Faust's child is no more than a magic prop used to conjure up the image of Helen of Troy. Throughout the entire course of the opera, Faust is shown to be a man of action, of will, whereas, Mephistopheles is a reactor to Faust's will. Mephistopheles' only hope for attaining Faust's soul, then, is not the contractual fulfillment of the pact but the containment of Faust's will to the acceptance of damnation. This Faust will not do, and during the transference of his vital essence to his son he states:

---

[15]Busoni, <u>Doktor Faust</u>, Vorspiel I, p. 13.

Blutes meines Blutes
Glied meines Gliedes,
Ungeweckter,
Geistig-reiner,
noch ausserhalb aller Kreife
und mir in diesem
innigst verwandt,
dir vermach' ich mein Leben:
es schreite
von der erdeingebissenen Wurzel
meiner scheidenden Zeit
in die luftig knospende Blüte
deines werwenden Seins.
So wirk' ich weiter in dir,
und du zeuge fort
und grabe tiefer und tiefer
die Spur meines Wesens
bis an das Ende des Triebes.
Was ich verbaute,
richte du grade
was ich versäumte,
schöpfe du nach,
so stell' ich mich
über die Regel
umfass in Einem
die Epochen
und vermenge mich
den letzten Geschlechtern:
ich, Faust,
ein ewiger Wille![16]

Busoni has replaced Goethe's "Ewig-Weibliche" with a self-transcending ego, a thoroughly modern Faust in no need of divine intercession or self-effacing love. Busoni's Faust is "saved" not because of a desire to do good works or a misconceived plan to improve the lot of others, but because of his desire to evolve into a higher being. Mephistopheles' final rhetorical question, "Sollte dieser Mann verunglückt sein?" must, therefore, be answered in the negative.

The chorus plays a very significant role in Doktor Faust, one that approaches the multiplicity of purposes that Goethe envisioned in his Faust. Initially, the chorus is heard intoning the Easter service which serves as an ironic background to the visit from the three students from

[16]Ibid., pp. 42-43.

Crakow, Faust's invocation of the Devil, and the signing of the pact. The infernal spirits as well as the soldiers who kill Valentine perform in choral fashion, with the result that the chorus becomes an active participant in the drama in addition to being a passive observer. Indeed, one can imagine a production of Doktor Faust in which the members of the chorus appear in several guises, much as Mephistopheles appears as himself, the herald, and the night watchman. The change in the appearance and purpose of the chorus is important for Busoni who, as will be seen below, is trying to posit a morality extending beyond the norms of good and evil. The chorus also appears as the guests and spectators at the Duke's wedding and as the group of students at the Tavern in Wittenberg. The latter is a remarkable scene in which the chorus, divided into opposing groups of Protestant and Catholic students, engages in a contrapuntally complex philosophical debate which ends inconclusively. This is an autobiographical detail, no doubt, of Busoni's own dual Germanic-Latin heritage. On another level this "debate" also serves as an ironic juxtaposition to Faust's infatuation with the apparition of Helen of Troy. The philosophical issues with which the students are grappling are of no importance to Faust who is concerned with Helen, the symbol of perfection at least in the aesthetic sense. It is precisely after Faust has failed in his attempt to grasp the vision of Helen that he rededicates his life to the attainment of the perfection symbolized by Helen, which makes the internecine theological squabbles of the students appear very insignificant:

> Ach, abermals betrogen!
> Verschwenden nun für immer!
> Der Mensch ist dem Vollkommenen
> nicht gewaschen.
> Er strebe denn
> nach seinem eigenen Masse
> und streue Gutes aus,
> wie es ihm gegeben.
> Ich weiser Narr,
> ich Säumer, ich Verschwender!
> Nichts ist getan,
> alles zu beginnen;
> der Kindheit fühl' ich wieder mich genähert.
> Weithin schaut auf mein junges
> Gelände,
> dort unbebaute Hügel, schwellendes Erdreich,

führen zu neuem Augstieg.
Wie verheissend lächelt das Leben
im erwachenden sonnelichten Tag![17]

Busoni's portrayal of Wagner is less that of the parvenu vainly attempting to replace Faust than as a rational and loyal assistant. At the beginning of the opera Wagner's limited perspective is exemplified by the fact that he is unable to see the three students from Crakow and is not aware that they have visited Faust. By the final scene Wagner has replaced Faust as Rector of the University but his remarks are not those of an unjustly promoted poseur; rather, they display real perspicacity as to the true nature of Faust: "...der Faust war mehr einem Phantasten; als Gelehrter nicht eigentlich vollwichtig...."[18] The implication of this is that at some time in the future Wagner may be able to attempt the same feat of self-transcendence that Faust has begun. Wagner's evolving perspective is a hopeful indication of a similar evolution of the will, which in Busoni's cosmos is the most important element for the development of the ego.

From the discussion above it should not be surprising that Busoni was profoundly influenced by the philosophy of Friedrich Nietzsche in the creation of Doktor Faust, particularly the concept of "die ewige Wiederkehr," whereby history is a succession of repetitions in which perfection is the ultimate goal. Many passages in the libretto display a remarkable similarity to portions of Beyond Good and Evil, none more so than several portions which have been omitted in the final version of the libretto as realized by Jarnach. In his very excellent biography Busoni the Composer, Anthony Beaumont provides the final lines of the libretto which were not set by Jarnach and which have been omitted from all published editions of the text since its premiere:

So let the Work be finished,
in defiance of you,
of you all,
who hold yourselves for good,
whom we call evil,
who, for the sake of old quarrels

---

[17]Ibid., pp. 36-37.
[18]Ibid., p. 39.

> take mankind as a pretext
> and pile upon him
> the consequence of your discord.
> Upon this highest insight of my wisdom
> is your malice now broken to pieces
> and in my self-won freedom
> expire both God and Devil at once.[19]

Probably no more explicit proclamation of the viability of the Übermensch exists in literature, and this omitted passage tellingly demonstrates the evolution of Faust as a seeker of knowledge at the beginning of the opera to the self-confident and self-actualized evolutionary being about to will his ego to a transcendent plane at the end of the work. Such an anti-Christian teleology may explain in part Jarnach's decision not to set these final lines of the libretto; however, on artistic grounds there is little to justify their omission inasmuch as they do not present a new perspective to Busoni's approach to the Faust legend, but rather reinforce that which has been apparent and manifest from the outset. In this regard I cannot agree with Beaumont's statement that "Nietzschean thought is buried deep in the personality of the composer and rises to the surface only at times of dire need...."[20] The influence of Nietzsche is apparent throughout the opera and is the single most important unifying feature of the composition. Viewed within the framework of Nietzsche's thought, Doktor Faust takes on a logical philosophical superstructure; without this influence the libretto seemingly becomes a series of phantasmagorical incidents, not unlike Lenau's Faust.[21]

---

[19]Anthony Beaumont, Busoni the Composer (Bloomington: Indiana University Press, 1985), p. 325.

[20]Ibid., p. 31.

[21]Certain textual features of Doktor Faust do bear a superficial similarity to sections of Lenau's Faust. Beaumont remarks (p. 323) that the original version of the libretto ended with the lines: "Ist das Leben nur ein Wahn/Was kann der Tod mehr sein?" This is somewhat analogous to Lenau's Faust remarking in his death scene as to the dream-like and solipsistic nature of life: "So ist's vielleicht dass Gott im Traume spürt,/ Er träume nur, und dass Erwachensdrang/Im Morgenschlaf an seinem Traume rührt?/Und schlummert er vielleicht nun nimmer lang?" (Nikolaus Lenau, Sämmtliche Werke [Leipzig: Reclam Verlag, 1883], p. 454). The difference between the two passages is that Lenau's Faust bemoans the falsity of existence, whereas Busoni's Faust looks upon the absurdity of this world as a clarion call for the will to manifest itself into a higher level of being, the ultimate act of bravery being the courage to face the unknown world of the transcendent ego.

At the beginning of the opera Faust is concerned with seeking knowledge and power, but implied in this desire is that the attainment of these goals will occur during Faust's lifetime. That is the whole purpose of the pact: a quid pro quo arrangement within a specified period of time. As the opera progresses it becomes apparent to Faust that his desires are incapable of being fulfilled; however, one possible course of action exists in the transference of his vital essence to the body of his dead son which he proceeds to do. By engaging in this action Faust is actively participating in the process of "eternal recurrence" and thereby transcends the temporality of both the Devil and God. Faust's final deed may be the desperate and uncertain action of a man attempting to cheat fate, but it is not out of keeping with other rash actions that Faust has perpetrated in earlier scenes (for Faust, as has already been shown, generally acts without considering the consequences). It is the uncertainty of the results of actions in Nietzsche's opinion that is necessary for the creation of the Übermensch via the eternal recurrence. In The Will to Power he states:

> To endure the idea of the [eternal] recurrence one needs: freedom from morality; new means against the fact of pain...; the enjoyment of all kinds of uncertainty, experimentation, as a counterweight to this extreme fatalism; abolition of the concept of necessity; abolition of the "will"; abolition of "knowledge-in-itself."[22]

Clearly, Faust's earlier experiences have been a preparation for his final act of transcendence and follow Nietzsche's prescription in this regard.

Faust's evolution from man to incipient Übermensch influences the entirety of Doktor Faust, which, overtly or subliminally, proceeds along a line of development anticipated by Nietzsche. This can be exemplified in several instances. First of all, Faust evolves from the seeker of knowledge (scholar) to the seeker of self-fulfillment (man of action). This was foreseen by Nietzsche as a necessary condition for the development of the Übermensch. According to Nietzsche, the scholar is incapable of self-actualization and enduring the uncertainty of the eternal recurrence:

[22]Friedrich Nietzsche, The Will to Power, translated by Walter Kaufmann and R.J. Hollingdale (New York: Vintage, 1967), pp. 545-46.

> Der objektive Mensch [scholar] is in der That ein Spiegel: vor Allem, was erkannt werden will, zur Unterwerfung gewohnt, ohne eine andre Lust, als wie sie das Erkennen, das "Abspiegeln" giebt, --er wartet, bis Etwas kommt, und breitet sich dann zart hin, dass auch leichte Fusstapfen und das Vorüberschlüpfen geisterhafter Wesen nicht auf seiner Fläche und Haut verloren gehen.[23]

Additionally, as remarked above, Faust's relationship to Mephistopheles undergoes a transformation from that of follower to ruler. In the end Faust has reduced Mephistopheles to the role of commentator. Faust's route to a higher level of being has been long and arduous, which is understandable according to Nietzsche: "Die seltsame Beschränktheit der menschlichen Entwicklung, das Zögernde, Langwierige, oft Zurücklaufende und Sich-Drehende derselben beruht darauf, dass der Heerden-Instinkt des Gehorsams am besten und auf Kosten der Kunst des Befehlens vererbt wird."[24]

The influence of Nietzsche in Doktor Faust extends to the eclecticism of Busoni's compositional style with its mixture of modern chromatic harmonies, baroque and classical forms, and the conspicuous features of the Faust Puppenspiel. This all-encompassing aspect of Busoni's method of composition, usually labelled by critics as atavistic or a manifestation of the "neoclassicism" of the 1920s, is, in reality, another version of Nietzsche's eternal recurrence, and as such, the music of Doktor Faust serves as a symbol of Nietzsche's most profound philosophical construction. It is Busoni's intention to abrogate the historicity of artistic forms, to embrace the concept of the eternal recurrence, that places his work within the vanguard of the modernist movement of the early 20th century. As Mircea Eliade has remarked:

---

[23]Friedrich Nietzsche, Jenseits von Gut und Böse: Vorspiel einer Philosophie der Zukunft (Leipzig: C.G. Naumann, 1891), p. 140. [Friedrich Nietzsche, Beyond Good and Evil: Prelude to a Philosophy of the Future, translated by Walter Kaufmann (New York: Vintage, 1966), pp. 126-27: "The objective man is indeed a mirror: he is accustomed to submit before whatever wants to be known, without any other pleasure than that found in knowing and "mirroring"; he waits until something comes, and then spreads himself out tenderly lest light footsteps and the quick passage of spiritual beings should be lost on his plane and skin."]

[24]Ibid., p. 119 [Kaufmann, p. 110: "The strange limits of human development, the way it hesitates, takes so long, often turns back, and moves in circles, is due to the fact that the herd instinct of obedience is inherited best, and at the expense of commanding."]

> ... [W]e noted various recent orientations that tend to reconfer value upon the myth of cyclical periodicity, even the myth of eternal return. These orientations disregard not only historicism but even history as such. We believe we are justified in seeing in them, rather than a resistance to history, a revolt against historical time, an attempt to restore this historical time, freighted as it is with human experience, to a place in the time that is cosmic, cyclical, and infinite. In any case it is worth noting that the work of two of the most significant writers of our day--T.S. Eliot and James Joyce--is saturated with nostalgia for the myth of eternal repetition and, in the last analysis, for the abolition of time.[25]

The abolition of time, the elimination of eschatology from history, is Busoni's most profound contribution to the evolution of the Faust legend. If the Faustian man is no longer subject to the temporality of this world (either satanic or divine), then the universe becomes subject to the instinctive creativity of his will. In 400 years we have come full circle: from the inevitability of Faust's damnation in the protestant platitudes of Johann Spies' Faustbuch to the inevitably repetitive Übermensch of the agnostic Busoni. And Busoni's vision of Faust may have more than an element of truth to it. In recent years a new concept of cosmological evolution, the anthropic principle, has been proposed which contends that the evolution of the universe is directly linked to the ability to perceive natural laws, that natural laws exist because they are perceived.[26] In this conception of the universe Faustian man is paramount; indeed, each step in the evolution of the universe can occur only after each step in the evolution of man. If this scientific theory is ever shown to be true, then Busoni will have the unique distinction as the only composer to have created a work not only representing one of the richest intellectual and artistic traditions of Western civilization, but of creation itself.

---

[25]Mircea Eliade, The Myth of the Eternal Return: or, Cosmos and History, translated by Willard R. Trask (Princeton: Princeton University Press, 1954), p. 153.

[26]See in particular Tony Rothman, "A 'What You See Is What You Beget' Theory" in Discover 8:5 (May 1987): 90-99.

CHAPTER V

Diabolus in musica: Thomas Mann's Doktor Faustus

> It is indeed difficult not to believe that the work
> of art has a metaphysical will of its own as it
> strives to come into being, regarding the life of
> its creator as a mere toll and sacrificial victim,
> half willing, half unwilling.
> --Thomas Mann, "The Sorrows and Grandeur
> of Richard Wagner"--

> Mediocrity, in fact, has no theological status.
> --Adrian Leverkühn--

Thomas Mann's great masterpiece, Doktor Faustus (1947), has produced more conflicting and contradictory interpretations than probably any other novel of the twentieth century, even including those of James Joyce and Samuel Beckett. Although much has been written about the use of music as a metaphor for German civilization and Adrian Leverkühn's illness as a synecdoche for that civilization's decline, very little attention has been paid to the seemingly deterministic nature of Mann's narrative. The inexorable progression of Leverkühn's disease is directly linked to the historical consequences of Nazi rule on a very broad level and the historical evolution of music on a smaller level. What is most fascinating in Mann's brilliant tri-partite temporal structuring is the historical inevitability of events, a coldly deterministic linkage of cause and effect, that impinges directly upon every element of the novel at both macrocosmic and microcosmic levels and produces a work unlike any in the long literary tradition of the Faust legend.

Historical determinism becomes very apparent early on in the novel in the section devoted to Leverkühn's youth and early adulthood. In fact, the course of Leverkühn's life seems predetermined almost from birth, and in this regard the protagonist is less a demonic personage himself than like a hero of Greek tragedy being led to the fulfillment of his fate.

Adrian's father, Jonathan Leverkühn, is described in Chapter III of the novel as a scientific dilettante whose primitive experiments occupy a position somewhat between science and alchemy. Although this chapter is generally regarded as background information for the development of the novel (with the exception of the butterfly haetera esmeralda which will be featured later on in the novel as both a literary and musical leitmotif), the nature of Jonathan's experimentation produces a profound effect on Adrian (even though this effect is not emphasized by Serenus Zeitblom, the accurate narrator with a severely limited perspective) and reinforces the idea that Adrian's artistic proclivities are the result of heredity instead of the will. In particular, Jonathan Leverkühn is occupied with ascertaining an inherent language in mollusk markings and in exploring the morphological symmetry of ice crystals and flowers, both of which are determined by nature.[1] There is a parallel between Jonathan's fascination with the predetermined structure of nature and Adrian's espousal of the musical 12-tone system in which the tonal aspect at least is determined before actual composition occurs. In addition, both Adrian and Jonathan suffer from migraines (physical suffering being a necessary condition in Mann's etiology of genius) which tends to support the link between father and son and is, no doubt, a foreshadowing of the greater physical suffering and acts of genius that will take place later in the life of Adrian.[2] In this regard, Jonathan Leverkühn appears as one of the many manifestations of the Devil, or perhaps, more accurately, one of the many manifestations of Adrian's daimon, the catalyst whose function it is to see that the protagonist's fate is fulfilled.

Adrian's hereditary proclivities are further reinforced by his uncle, Nikolaus Leverkühn, with whom he lives during his gymnasium years. Nikolaus, the proprietor of a musical instrument firm and a violin-maker by trade (the violin, of course, being the "Devil's instrument"), provides encouragement and virtually unlimited resources for Adrian's burgeoning

---

[1]Thomas Mann, Doktor Faustus: Das Leben des deutschen Tonsetzers Adrian Leverkühn erzählt von einem Freunde (Frankfurt a.M.: Fischer Bücherei, 1967), pp. 21-22 . [Translation by H.T. Lowe-Porter, New York: Vintage Books 1948, pp. 17-18.]

[2]It is important to note that Adrian's migraines and his interest in music begin at the same time, i.e., about the onset of puberty.

interest in music. It is during this extended period of residence at his uncle's home in Kaisersaschern that two of Adrian's other interests become apparent, namely, mathematics and religion.

Mathematics is especially important in Leverkühn's development as a composer because it is through his experimentation with numerical properties of harmony (e.g., the circle of fifths) that the first inkling of the dodecaphonic system becomes evident:

> Und er [Leverkühn] liess einem Akkord ertönen, lauter schwarze Tasten, fis, ais, cis, fügte ein e hinzu und demonskierte dadurch den Akkord, der wie Fis-Dur ausgesehen hatte, als zu H-Dur gehörig, nämlich als dessen fünfte oder Dominant-Stufe. "So ein Zusammenklang," meinte er, "hat an sich keine Tonart. Alles ist Beziehung, und die Beziehung bildet den Kreis." Das a, welches, indem es die Auflösung in gis erzwingt, von H- nach E-Dur überleitet, führte ihn weiter, und so kann er über A-, D- und G- nach C-Dur und in die mit Verminderungszeichen, versehen Tonarten, indem er mir demonstrierte, dass man auf einem jeden der zwölf Töne der chromatischen Leiter eine eigene Dur- oder Moll-Skala errichten könne.[3]

Clearly, Leverkühn sees an organic relationship among the twelve steps of the chromatic scale which is rooted in the circle of fifths. Throughout music history, however, many theorists (particularly Jean-Philippe Rameau, Paul Hindemith, and Heinrich Schenker) have looked upon the circle of fifths as conforming to natural laws, in other words, a tonal system obeying laws of causation and effect as predetermined as the Newtonian laws

---

[3]Mann, P. 49 [Lowe-Porter, p. 46: And he played a chord: all black keys, F sharp, A sharp, C sharp, added an E, and so unmasked the chord, which had looked like F-sharp major, as belonging to B major, as its dominant. "Such a chord," he said, "has of itself no tonality. Everything is relation, and the relation forms the circle." The A, which, forcing the resolution into G sharp, leads over from B major to E major, led him on, and so via the keys of A, D, and G he came to C major and to the flat keys, as he demonstrated to me that on each one of the twelve notes of the chromatic scale one could build a fresh major or minor scale.]

governing motion and thermodynamics.[4] The natural law implication of the above discourse is given credence by Leverkühn's statement that:

> Die Ordnug ist alles. Römer dreizehn: 'Was von Gott ist, das ist geordnet.'[5]

It is here that the connection between music and religion becomes apparent, a synthesis, as it were, of Pythagoreanism and medieval Christianity. As theology imparts an organized and systematic view of the cosmos, and as mathematics requires the systematic ordering of postulates and proofs, so too does Leverkühn find a natural order inherent in the tonal system: "Weisst du, was ich finde?" fragte er [Leverkühn]. "Dass Musik die Zweideutigkeit ist als System."[6]

The above statement seems innocent enough, yet it is remarkable in that Leverkühn asserts that music imposes order from within, that music obeys laws of its own making rather than being subject to the conscious form-making decisions of cultural selectivity. The composer in Leverkühn's cosmos is less of a tonal decision maker than a discoverer of principles already inherent in the sonic materials with which he is working. This approach to artistic creativity is very similar to the theological adumbration of revealed wisdom and the scientist's quest for unified and universal laws of natural phenomena.

Adrian Leverkühn's <u>daimon</u> appears in many guises but perhaps never more significantly than in the being of Wendell Krestzschmar, the American expatriate music master and Leverkühn's only real teacher of

---

[4]For an explanation of the concept of the "natural" scale evolving from the circle of fifths (which was rooted in overtone theory) see Richard Norton's brilliant study, <u>Tonality in Western Culture: A Critical and Historical Perspective</u> (University Park: The Pennsylvania State University Press, 1984). On page 34 Norton remarks: "The 'natural' superiority of the intervallic fifth, secured by the overtone series for both Rameau and Schenker, obviates any critical examination of the scale as a theoretically stated tonal substance. The major scale is simply taken to be the expression of the system's root tones which have obeyed the laws of fifth evolution."

[5]Mann, p. 48. [Lowe-Porter, p. 45: Order is everything. Romans xiii: 'For there is no power but of God: the powers that be are ordained of God.']

[6]Mann, p. 50. [Lowe-Porter, p. 47: 'You know what I find?' he (Leverkühn) asked. 'That music turns the equivocal into a system.']

composition.[7] Kretzschmar's significance as a daimon extends not only to Leverkühn's choice of career as a composer--it is Kretzschmar who ultimately supplies Adrian with the justification to abandon theological studies and return to music--but also to the course that Adrian's musical career will follow.

Kretzschmar's musical influence over Leverkühn is more philosophical in nature than pedagogical (Leverkühn, like Joseph Haydn, being the most serious of autodidacts). It is Kretzschmar's insistence on the advisability and historical inevitability of musical "objectivity" (i.e., determinism) that points Leverkühn in the direction of dodecaphonic music, the quintessence of objective and deterministic musical forms. The most explicit example of this type of musical theorizing is seen in Kretzschmar's lecture-recital concerning Beethoven's Op. 111 C Minor Piano Sonata which is found in Chapter VIII of the novel.

In the sparsely attended lecture-recital in the Hall of the Society of Activities for the Common Weal, Kretzschmar begins his discussion of Op. 111 by pointing out the inability of Beethoven's contemporaries to fathom the direction in which the composer was taking the piano sonata. Indeed, this was the general feeling about Beethoven's late period compositions which is confirmed in the following contemporary review of Op. 111 in the Berlin Allgemeine musikalische Zeitung:

> Perhaps you, dear Editor, can establish a position from which criticism and the commonly accepted rules of aesthetics can be defended against these novelties, these attacks upon first principles. For when the primary conception of a work of art

---

[7]Kretzschmar is a thinly disguised composite portrait of the philosopher T.W. Adorno and the music historian Hermann Kretzschmar with some of the biographical details and personality characteristics of Friedrich Nietzsche as well. Another possible model for Wendell Kretzschmar is the minor German composer Edmund Kretschmer whose biography bears many resemblances to that created by Mann for his fictitious music master. Another interesting detail is that Wendell Kretzschmar is a native of Pennsylvania of "Pennsylvania Dutch" extraction who decides to settle in the land of his forebears. Although this detail is ostensibly meant to strengthen the force of Kretzschmar's discussion of Conrad Beissel's musical experiments at the Ephrata Cloister, there is a slight possibility that Kretzschmar is an oblique reference to Nikolaus Lenau, the author of a very famous Faust of 1833 (and one of the subjects of Chapter I of this book) who lived in Pennsylvania and Ohio for approximately one year at settlements founded by German Pietists and who eventually returned to his native Austria.

is divorced from reason, when feeling alone determines every basis for judgment, when works that scorn all our rules gain such passionate admirers--then I must be silent.[8]

The subjectivity of Beethoven's highly idiosyncratic approach to the sonata is mitigated, in Kretzschmar's opinion, by the utilization of conventional compositional techniques (e.g., the theme and variations form) which are developed to the point of exhaustion. The transformation of the subjective/personally expressive to that of the objective/transcendent is made possible by the proximity of death, which in Beethoven's case is represented by the inexorable decay of his aural faculties. Therefore, the objectivity resulting from sickness and the nearness of death grants creative artists distance from their egos, a transcendence of the individual as it were, which is reflected in the transcendence of artistic forms from the conventional to the suprarational or "spiritual."

Leaving aside matters of artistic sickness and health, Mann's most pressing concern is to make a distinction between subjective and objective art because Op. 111 is described as objective, while Mann considers the works of Beethoven's middle period (ca. 1803-1815) to be subjective in orientation.[9] That aspect of Op. 111 (and by extension, the majority of compositions of Beethoven's late period) which allows it to move from the subjective realm to that of the objective is Beethoven's preoccupation with counterpoint. After establishing the subjective/ homophonic--objective/ contrapuntal dichotomy Mann effectively negates his argument in the following passage:

> Denn mit der Idee des nur Persönlichen verbinde man diejenige der schrankenlosen Subjektivität und des radikalen harmonischen Ausdruckswillens im Gegensatz zur polyphonischen Objektivität (er wünschte, wir möhten uns den Unterschied einprägen: harmonische Subjektivität, polyphonische Sachlichkeit), -- und diese Gleichung, diese

---

[8]No author given <u>Allgemeine musikalische Zeitung</u> 1 (1824): 99
[9]Mann, p. 55 [Lowe-Porter, p. 53]

Gegensatz wollten hier, wie beim meisterlichen Spätwerk
überhaupt, nicht stimmen. [emphasis mine] [10]

Taken as a whole, the late works of Beethoven are much more
contrapuntal than those of his middle period, and the contrast of
homophonic-contrapuntal construction (regardless of the applicability of
the subjective-objective components) is most useful and is something that
is utilized by almost every musicologist who studies Beethoven. If, for the
sake of argument, we agree that homophony is subjective and
counterpoint is objective, Kretzschmar needs to go no further in his
argument because the increasing contrapuntal complexity of Beethoven's
late works is palpable and easily verifiable. Mann has created a cultural
paradigm in contrapuntal complexity, peremptorily abandoned it in favor of
necrological objectivity, and still arrived at the same conclusion offered by
the original paradigm.

Inherent in Mann's argument that counterpoint is objective in nature
is the idea of contrapuntal determinism, i.e., that contrapuntal processes
are more subject to their inherent realizations than to the subjective
creativity of composers. Homophonic music, on the other hand, is
subjective by this line of reasoning precisely because of the relative
freedom it affords composers. On the simplest level, counterpoint is by no
means exempt from the subjectivity of creative fancy. The construction of
a fugue theme or the selection of a cantus firmus is a subjective
compositional decision. Likewise, the selection of a canon (i.e., the interval
of imitation, the point of imitation, the method of imitation [augmentation,
diminution, cancrizans, etc.] and the number of voices involved) and the
selection between imitative and non-imitative types of counterpoint are
subjective decisions and reflect the compositional proclivities of the
composer. Once a contrapuntal procedure has been initiated there are still

---

[10]Ibid., p. 55 [Lowe-Porter, pp. 52-53: For one would usually connect with the
conception of the merely personal, ideas of limitless subjectivity and of radical harmonic
will to expression, in contrast to polyphonic objectivity (Kretzschmar was concerned to
have us impress upon our minds this distinction between harmonic subjectivity and
polyphonic objectivity) and this equation, this contrast, here as altogether in the late
masterly works, would simply not apply. {emphasis mine}]

ample opportunities for the individual manifestation of the composer's stylistic idiosyncrasies.

Classical homophony, on the other hand, was not an entirely subjective type of music in which the composer possessed complete freedom. A type of musical grammar existed in the classical style in which homophonic music was made sensible by formulaic progressions of chords (cadences) not only delineating the phrase structure, but also establishing a means for modulating to different tonal areas. The conventional and "non-subjective" nature of classical homophony with regards to its emphasis upon cadences has been remarked upon with persuasive eloquence by Charles Rosen:

> ...[T]he classical style needed more forceful means of emphasizing new keys than the Baroque, and it used for this purpose a quantity of 'filling' almost unparalleled until then in the history of music except in pieces of an improvisatory character. By 'filling' I mean purely conventional material, superficially unrelated to the content of the piece, and apparently (and in some cases, actually) transferable bodily from one work to another. Every musical style, naturally, relies on conventional material, principally at cadences, which almost always follow traditional formulas. The classical style, however, further magnified and elongated the cadence in order to strengthen the modulation.[11]

Kretzschmar's insistence that Beethoven's use of "bald conventions" gives Op. 111 an aura of objectivity seems to be insupportable and is more likely the result of the standard stylistic procedures (and 'filling' procedures) peculiar to classical music.

What Mann has done here so brilliantly is to reduce Beethoven's individuality and greatness to an exalted but inevitable stage in an eschatological process that will eventually subsume Leverkühn's genius in a like manner. Kretzschmar as daimon transfers his powers in such a way that Beethoven becomes Leverkühn's daimon, an invisible yet everpresent representative of the historical apparatus compelling Adrian in his artistic endeavors. Beethoven's Op. 111, the "end without any return," the

---

[11]Charles Rosen, The Classical Style: Haydn, Mozart, Beethoven (New York: W.W. Norton & Co., 1972), p. 71.

quintessentially objective transcendence of sonata form, becomes a precursor of Leverkühn's 12-tone objectivity. Both of these "diseased" composers are virtually compelled to the creation of their "breakthrough" compositions in Kretzschmar's version of music history. Kretzschmar claims that music is the most intellectual of the arts and goes on to state:

> Allein an die Sinneswelt gebunden, müsse sie doch auch wieder nach stärkster, ja berückender Versinnlichung streben, eine Kundry, die nicht wolle, was sie tue [emphasis mine], und weiche Arme der Lust um den Nacken dies Toren schlinge.[12]

Kretzschmar's relating of Conrad Beissel's musical experiments at the Ephrata Cloister serves a similar purpose which, in turn, reinforces the links between music and religion, and musical determinism and religious eschatology. Beissel's pre-arranged ordering of chord progressions in his Turtletaube reflects a cosmic ordering that refers back to Pythagoreanism and medieval concepts concerning the music of the spheres. It is precisely this combination of musical, religious, and mathematical reasoning that appeals to Leverkühn:

> "Lass mir," sagte er [Leverkühn to Zeitblom],..."lass mir den Kauz [Beissel] in Frieden, ich habe was für ihn übrig. Wenigstens hatte er Ordnungssin, und sogar eine alberne Ordnung ist immer noch besser als gar keine."[13]

In Doktor Faustus Mann constantly provides biographical details of Leverkühn's life that run concurrently with the philosophical and analytical passages for which the novel is best known. The biographical details are laden with an aura of determinism that reflects the novel's preoccupation with artistic objectivity and sublimation of the individual will to historical processes: in other words, fictional art imitating fictional life. Concerning

---

[12]Mann, p. 64. [Lowe-Porter, p. 61: But bound as she was to the world of sense, music must ever strive after the strongest, yes, the most seductive sensuous realization: she is a Kundry, who wills not what she does [emphasis mine] and flings soft arms of lust round the neck of the fool.]

[13]Ibid., p. 71. [Lowe-Porter, pp. 67-68: "Leave me alone," he said [Leverkühn to Zeitblom],..."leave me in peace with my old codger [Beissel], I can do with him. At least he had a sense of order, and even a silly order is better than none at all."]

theology as Leverkühn's original choice as a course of study and the later
return to music, Zeitblom states:

> Hat Kaisersaschern ihn jemals freigegeben? Hat er es nicht
> mit sich genommen, wohin immer er ging, und ist er nicht
> von ihn bestimmt worden, wann immer er zu bestimmen
> glaubte? Was ist Freiheit? Nur das Gleichgültige ist frei. Das
> Charakteristische ist niemals frei, es ist geprägt, determiniert
> und gebunden. War es nicht "Kaisersaschern," was aus
> meines Freundes Entschlusse sprach, Theologie zu
> studieren? Adrian Leverkühn und diese Stadt, --gewiss, das
> ergab zusammen wohl Theologie; nachträglich fragte ich
> mich, was ich denn sonst erwartet hatte. Er widmete sich
> später der Komposition. Aber wenn es sehr kühne Musik
> war, die er schrieb, --war es etwa "freie" Musik,
> Allerweltsmusik? Das war es nicht. Es war die Musik eines
> nie Entkommenen, war bis in die geheimste genialisch--
> skurrile Verflechtung hinein, in jedem Kryptenhall und -hauch,
> der davon ausging charakteristische Musik, Musik von
> Kaisersaschern.--[14]

Even Leverkühn's personal idiosyncrasies appear to be determined
from birth. Zeitblom remarks that Adrian's laughter, which manifests itself
at seemingly inopportune moments, had an effect similar to that of "Cham,
der Sohn des Noah und Vater Zoroasters, des Magiers, der einzige
Mensch gewesen sei, der bei seiner Geburt gelacht habe, was nur mit Hilfe
des Teufels habe geschehen können."[15]

Adrian's years of theological study at the University of Halle cause
him to be influenced by several versions of his daimon. Professor Kolonat
Nonnenmacher instructs Leverkühn in Pythagorean philosophy and

---

[14]Ibid., p. 85. [Lowe-Porter, p. 83: Had Kaisersaschern ever released him? Did he
not take her with him wherever he went and was he not conditioned by her whenever he
thought to decide? What is freedom? Only the neutral is free. The characteristic is never
free, it is stamped, determined, bound. Was it not "Kaisersaschern" that spoke in my
friend's decision to study theology? Adrian Leverkühn and Kaisersaschern: obviously the
two together yielded theology. I asked myself further what else I had expected. He
devoted himself later to musical composition. But if it was very bold music he wrote, was it
after all "free" music, world music? That it was not. It was the music of one who never
escaped; it was, into its most mysterious, inspired, bizarre convolution, in every hollow
breath and echo it gave out, characteristic music, music of Kaisersaschern.]

[15]Ibid., p. 87. [Lowe-Porter, p. 85: Ham, son of Noah and father of Zoroaster the
magician, [who] had been the only man who laughed when he was born--which could only
have happened by the help of the Devil.]

reinforces Adrian's long-held fascination with an ordered cosmos, particularly one susceptible to mathematical reduction. Nonnenmacher's lectures also deal with Aristotelian philosophy and stress the philosopher's views on the inherent drive to the fulfillment of organic forms, in other words, the urge toward the unfolding of destiny. These lectures have a profound impact on Leverkühn who comes to the realization that his personal destiny is not necessarily of his own making and who obliquely remarks:

> "Wenn," sagte er [Leverkühn], "die Theologie erklärt, dass die Seele von Gott sei, so ist das philosophisch richtig, denn als das Prinzip, das die Einzelerscheinungen formt, ist sie ein Teil der reinen Form alles Seins überhaupt, entstammt dem ewig sich selbst denkenden Denken, das wir 'Gott' nennen.... Ich glaube zu verstehen, was Aristoteles mit der Entelechie meinte. Sie ist der Engel des Einzelwesens, der Genius seines Lebens, auf dessen wissende Führung es gern vertraut.[16]

Adrian's <u>daimon</u> finds a different and more subtle version in the form of Ehrenfried Kumpf, Mann's caricature of Martin Luther. Kumpf's theology rejects humanism and reason and embraces a rather lusty appreciation of life, including its sensual pleasures of which music is but one facet. Although Kumpf is a minor figure in the novel, his influence is long lasting on Adrian who adopts the former's archaic German phraseology and syntax and who eventually abandons the rationality and "coldness" of theology for the "warmth" of music.

Of all of Adrian's professors at Halle none leaves a more permanent impression and is more overtly a manifestation of Leverkühn's <u>daimon</u> than Eberhard Schleppfuss, the mysterious theologian whose very difficult lectures combine the tenets of Christianity with a blatant manicheanism.

---

[16]<u>Ibid</u>., p. 96. [Lowe-Porter, p. 94: "When," he [Leverkühn] said, "theology declares that the soul is from God, that is philosophically right, for as the principle which shapes the single manifestations, it is a part of the pure form of all being, comes from the eternally self-contemplating contemplation which we shall call God.... I believe I understand what Aristotle meant by the word 'entelechy.' It is the angel of the individual, the genius of his life, in whose all-knowing guidance it gladly confides."]

84

Schleppfuss views Evil as a necessary concomitant to Good and posits a sinister interpretation of the nature of creativity:

> Ihm zufolge war dies alles, war das Böse, war der Böse selbst ein notwendiger Ausfluss und ein unvermeidliches Zubehör der heiligen Existenz Gottes selbst; wie denn auch das Laster nicht aus sich selbst bestand, sondern seine Lust aus der Besuldelung der Tugend zog, ohne welche es wurzellos gewesen wäre; anders gesagt: es bestand in dem Genuss der Freiheit, das heisst der Möglichkeit, zu sündigen, <u>die dem Schöpfungsakt selbst inhärent war</u> [emphasis mine].... Das logische Dilemma Gottes hatte darin bestanden, dass er ausserstande gewesen war, dem Geschöpf, dem Menschen und den Engeln, zugleich die Selbstständigkeit der Wahl, also freien Willen, und die Gabe zu verleihen;, nicht sündigen zu können. Frömmigkeit und Tugend bestanden also darin, von der Freiheit, die Gott dem Geschöpf als solchem hatte gewähren müssen, einen guten Gebrauch, das heisst: <u>keinen</u> Gebrauch zu machen,--was nun freilich, wenn man Schleppfuss hörte, ein wenig so herauskam, als ob dieser Nicht-Gebrauch der Freiheit eine gewisse existentielle Abschwächung, eine Minderung der Daseinintensität der aussergöttlichen Kreatur bedeute.[17]

This is very similar to the Kierkegaardian conception of genius being <u>ipso facto</u> sinful. One born with genius, with the need to exercise creative freedom, would therefore be born with sin and, by logical extension, would be condemned to damnation from birth. Ironically, by this line of reasoning, Leverkühn could be "saved" only by the abnegation of that gift which by theological standards is most symbolic of man's creation in the image of God. Leverkühn's existential dilemma is such that Schleppfuss'

---

[17]<u>Ibid.</u>, pp. 101-2. [Lowe-Porter, pp. 100-101: According to Schleppfuss all this--evil, the Evil One himself--was a necessary emanation and inevitable accompaniment of the Holy Existence of God, so that vice did not consist in itself but got its satisfaction from the defilement of virtue, without which it would have been rootless; in other words, it consisted in the enjoyment of freedom, the possibility of sinning, <u>which was inherent in the act of creation itself</u> [emphasis mine].... God's logical dilemma had consisted in this: that He had been incapable of giving the creature, the human being and the angel, both independent choice, in other words free will, and at the same time the gift of not being able to sin. Piety and virtue, then, consisted in making a good use, that is to say no use at all, of the freedom which God had to grant the creature as such--and that, indeed, if you listened to Schleppfuss, was a little as though this non-use of freedom meant a certain existential weakening, a diminution of the intensity of being, in the creature outside of God.]

theology does not permit the choice of Good over Evil: "Freiheit ist die
Freiheit zu sündigen, Frömmigkeit besteht darin, von der Freiheit aus Liebe
zu Gott, der sie geben musste, keinen Gebrauch zu machen."[18] The
exercise of free will ultimately will prove to be of no avail for Leverkühn
since the possibility of choosing an alternative course does not exist.

From an intellectual standpoint, Schleppfuss' theology leads to a
dead end which is recognized by Leverkühn. The recognition of this leads
Leverkühn not away from the realm of inherently sinful creation but
precisely back to the field of musical composition. Schleppfuss as daimon
has accomplished his task by demonstrating to Leverkühn the impossibility
of the positive use of freedom. Since the individual will is obviated by a
pervasive determinism Leverkühn resolves to seek individually-
transcending objectivity which is more an inherent function of music than
theology. Speaking to his former theology classmates about his decision
to abandon his studies at Halle, Leverkühn remarks about the subjective
nature of theology:

> Ich habe eine Ahnung, dass ich es auch in der Kirche nicht
> weit bringen werde, aber gewiss ist, dass ich ohne sie nicht
> Theolog geworden wäre. Ich weiss ja, dass es die
> Begabtesten von euch sind, die Kierkegaard gelesen haben,
> die Wahrheit, auch die ethische Wahrheit, ganz ins Subjektive
> verlegen und alles Herdendasein perhorreszieren. Aber ich
> kann euren Radikalismus, der übrigens bestimmt nicht lange
> vorhalten wird, der eine Studentenlizenz ist,--ich kann euere
> Kierkegaardsche Trennung von Kirche und Christentum nicht
> mitmarchen. Ich sehe in der Kirche auch noch, wie sie heute
> ist, säkularisiert und verbürgerlicht, eine Burg ist Ordnung,
> eine Anstalt zur objektiven Disziplinierung, Kanalisierung,
> Eindämmung des religiösen Lebens, das ohne sie der
> subjektivistischen Verwilderung, den numinosen Chaos
> verfiele, zu einer Welt phantastischer Unheimlichkeit, einem
> meer von Dämonie würde. Kirche und Religion zu trennen,
> heisst darauf versichten, das Religiöse vom Wahnsinn zu
> trennen...."[19]

---

[18]Ibid., p. 103. [Lowe-Porter, p. 102: Freedom is the freedom to sin, and piety consists
in making no use of it out of love for God, who had to give it.]

[19]Ibid., pp. 120-21. [Lowe-Porter, p. 119: I have a feeling that I shan't go very far in the
Church either; but one thing is certain, that I should not have become a theologian without
her. I know of course that it is the most talented among you, those who have read
Kierkegaard, who place truth, even ethical truth, entirely in the subjective, and reject with
horror everything that savours of her existence. But I cannot go with you in your

· Like Wendell Kretzschmar's advocacy of "objective" counterpoint over "subjective" harmony, Leverkühn's embracing of the "objective" church in place of the "subjective" field of theology reflects less of an individual choice than a realization of the futility of human freedom and the necessity to abide by the inevitable and predetermined course of historical development.

Leverkühn's return to musical studies is commented upon by Zeitblom in such a way as to emphasize Adrian's return to the fulfillment of his destiny:

> Ich spürte, nicht ohne Beklemmung, einen Schicksalsabgrund [emphasis mine] zwischen dieser strebend gehobenen Jugend [Leverkühn's fellow theology students] und seiner [Leverkühn's] Existenz, den Unterschied der Lebenskurve zwischen gutem, ja vortrefflichem Durchschnitt, dem bald aus dem vagierenden, versuchenden Burschentum ins bürgerliche Leben einzulenken bestimmt war, und dem unsichtbar Gezeichneten [emphasis mine], der den Weg des Geists und der Problematik nie verlassen, ihn wer weiss wohin weitergehen sollte, und dessen Blick, dessen nie ganz ins Brüderliche sich lösende Haltung, dessen Hemmungen beim Du--und Ihr--und Wir--Sagen mich und wahrscheinlich auch die anderen empfinden liess, dass auch er diesen Unterschied ahnte.[20]

---

radicalism--...I cannot go with you in your separation, after Kierkegaard, of Church and Christianity. I see in the Church...a citadel of order, an institution of objective, disciplining, canalizing, banking-up of the religious life, which without her would fall victim to subjectivist demoralization, to a chaos of divine and daemonic powers, to a world of fantastic uncanniness, an ocean of daemony. To separate Church and religion means to give up separating the religious from madness.]

[20]Ibid., p. 127. [Lowe-Porter, p. 126: I felt, not without a pang, the foreordained gulf [emphasis mine] between his [Leverkühn's] existence and that of these striving and high-purposed youths [Leverkühn's fellow theology students]. It was the difference of the life-curve between good, yet, excellent average, which was destined to return from that roving, seeking student life to its bourgeois courses, and the other, invisibly singled out [emphasis mine], who would never forsake the hard route of the mind, would tread it, who knew whither, and whose gaze, whose attitude, never quite resolved in the fraternal, whose inhibitions in his personal relations made me and probably others aware that he himself divined this difference.]

Self-realization appears to be the single most important lesson of Adrian's years of study at Halle, and this serves to reinforce artistic and intellectual tendencies that were present at a very early age. Concerning the culmination of his theological studies, Leverkühn says that "...Musik immer als eine magische Verbindung aus Theologie und der so unterhaltenden Mathematik erschienen,"[21] a remark displaying the protagonist's conscious knowledge of a fact that readers of the novel had long known him to possess on an intuitive level.

It is abundantly clear that Leverkühn's reawakened interest in music takes into account his earlier mathematical and theological studies. Adrian acknowledges an appreciation of the Ptolemaic or "natural" scale and links this to Ptolemy's astronomical studies,[22] thereby providing an analogy to the concept of the music of the spheres which implies a natural deterministic order to the construction of the major mode. Similarly, Adrian expresses a preference for counterpoint over the purely harmonic aspect of music and describes the former as a "Zauberfelde" in a letter to Kretzschmar.[23]

Leverkühn's involvement with music is made permanent, however, only after the liaison with the prostitute Esmeralda which, interestingly enough, occurs after Adrian has witnessed the Austrian premiere of Richard Strauss' opera Salome based on Oscar Wilde's visionary Decadent drama. This liaison is a curious phenomenon in that neither lust nor intellectual curiosity appear to be its root cause. In many ways Adrian is as irresistibly drawn to the prostitute Esmeralda as the symbolic butterfly hetaera esmeralda of Chapter II is susceptible to visual or olfactory stimuli. There is a certain inevitability in both cases in which moral laws and the individual will are transcended by reflex actions firmly based in the instinctive domain. Additionally, Adrian's brief sexual encounter permits the appearance in rapid succession of two other manifestations of his daimon, namely Drs. Erasmi and Zimbalist, both of whom are thwarted (in

---

[21]Ibid., p. 132. [Lowe-Porter, p. 131: "...music has always seemed to me personally a magic marriage between theology and the diverting mathematic."]

[22]Ibid., pp. 159-60. [Lowe-Porter, p. 160.]

[23]Ibid., p. 141. [Lowe-Porter, p. 140.]

coincidences worthy of the melodramatic) from treating Adrian's syphilis in its incipient stage.

Adrian's fall is akin to the fall of Adam; both are terrible yet necessary for the evolution of the human condition. One can no more imagine a Christian eschatology without Adam's transgression than a continuation of musical evolution beyond Wagner without the imposition of a seminal figure such as Leverkühn (or, in reality, Schönberg).[24] The connection between Adrian and Adam is further strengthened by the fact that one of Leverkühn's first mature works is a setting of William Blake's poem "A Poison Tree" with its references to the poisoned fruit and the serpent who despoils an altar.

Adrian's choice of Blake--indeed, his fascination with English literary sources--is influenced by his strong friendship with Rüdiger Schildknapp, a translator and anglophile. There is a strong affinity between the composer and littérateur; the latter, like Leverkühn, is a diseased artist suffering from catarrh of the bladder and the two men share the same color of eyes, a condition that Mann often provides for the various manifestations of Adrian's daimon.

It is at this point in the novel that Mann's analogy among the "demonic" artistic decline of German music in general and of Leverkühn in particular with the impending demonic collapse of Nazi Germany becomes very strained. The inspiration that English literature (ranging from Shakespeare to Blake) holds for Leverkühn tends to negate the analogy of the demonic with the Germanic; however, Mann may be trying to infer subtly that Leverkühn's inherently demonic nature has the power to cause his sources to descend into the realm of the demonic regardless of their national origins.

The descriptions of Leverkühn's compositional style show the composer to be less concerned with artistic originality than in continuing processes initiated by earlier composers going back as far as J.S. Bach

---

[24]The necessity of progressing beyond Wagner is made obliquely by Leverkühn as related by Zeitblom (p. 163): "Schliesslich sei es doch wahr, dass die ganze deutsche Musikentwicklung zu dem Wort-Ton-Drama Wagners hinstrebe und ihr Ziel darin finde." [Lowe-Porter, p. 164: "Finally it was a fact that the whole development of music in Germany strove towards the word-tone drama of Wagner and therein found its goal."]

and Mozart. In fact, Leverkühn's basic artistic tendencies are described in terms quite reminiscent of the usual stylistic descriptions of 18th-century musical classicism. As Zeitblom relates:

> Das Element eines zum Äussersten gehenden Ausdruckswillens war immer herrschend in ihm [Leverkühn], zusammen mit der intellektuellen Leidenschaft für herbe Ordnung, das niederländisch Lineare. Mit anderen Worten: Hitze und Kälte walteten nebeneinander in seinem Werk, und zuweilen, in den genialsten Augenblicken, schlugen sie ineinander, das Espressivo ergriff den strikten Kontrapunkt, das Objektive rötete sich von Gefühl, so dass man den Eindruck einer glühenden Konstruktion hatte, die mir, wie nichts anderes, die Idee des Dämonischen nahebrachte....[25]

Why should this almost Mozartean balance between expression and form, between homophony and counterpoint, strike Zeitblom as the quintessence of the demonic? It is precisely because the naive narrator of the novel has unwittingly revealed that it is music ipso facto (specifically German music) that is demonic in nature and that previous generations of German composers differ in the demonic aspect of their compositions from that found in Leverkühn's work in degree but not in kind. By Zeitblom's reasoning the very ideal of classical balance and symmetry is opposed to the natural state of music and is an imposition of the artistic will which is perforce demonically inspired. Zeitblom further states that:

> ...der der eigentliche Anwalt der Werk-Idee ist, --nicht der Idee eines Werkes, sondern der Idee des Opus selbst, des in sich ruhenden, objektiven und harmonischen Gebildes überhaupt,--der Manager seiner Geschlossenheit, Einheit, Organik, der Risse verklebt, Löscher stopft jenen "natürlich Fluss" zuwege bringt, der ursprünglich nicht vorhanden war, und also gar nicht natürlich, sondern ein Kunstprodukt ist,--

---

[25]Mann, p. 178. [Lowe-Porter, p. 178: Always dominant in him [Leverkühn] was a will to go to extremes of expression; together with the intellectual passion for austere order, the linear style of the Netherlands composers. In other words, heat and cold prevail alongside each other in his work; sometimes in moments of the greatest genius they play into each other, the espressivo takes hold of the strict counterpoint, the objective blushes with feeling. One gets the impression of a glowing mould; this, like nothing else, has brought home to me the idea of the demonic.]

kurz, nachträglich erst und mittelbar stellt dieser Manager den Eindruck des Unmittelbaren und Organischen her.[26]

In other words, that music which has been regarded by generations of audiences as the most natural and balanced--in fact, that music which has been accepted within the limited and moralistic parameters of the bourgeois canon--is infected with the same demonic tendencies as the avant-garde compositions of Leverkühn. This point is brought out by the fact that Adrian takes great pains to justify his 12-tone method as an extension of previous musical innovations.

There are allusions to three historical sources for Leverkühn's 12-tone method. The first of these is the Wagnerian concept of dichterische Absicht, that is, where the poetic intention of the text can be realized fully only through music and which in large part determines the form and content of the music. Speaking of Leverkühn's 13 Brentano songs, Zeitblom states:

> Et war die Musik,...die mich zu der Gabe vermochte [an original edition of Brentano poems given to Leverkühn by Zeitblom],--die Musik, die in diesen Versen in so leichtem Schlummer liegt, dass die leiseste Behührung von berufener Hand genügte, sie zu erwecken.[27]

The second of the historical sources is the concept of the developing variations which was first promulgated by Arnold Schönberg as a means to describe the organic thematicism found in the music of Johannes Brahms. In the following quotation, Leverkühn places Brahms within the historical context of Beethoven's late style as described by Kretzschmar in Chapter VIII:

---

[26]Ibid., pp. 180-81. [Lowe-Porter, p. 180: ...the understanding which is the actual agent of the work-idea--not the idea of a particular work but the idea of opus itself, the objective and harmonic creation complete, the manager of its unified organic nature, which sticks the cracks together, stops up the holes, brings out that "natural flow"--which was not there in the first place and so is not natural at all, but a product of art--in short, only in retrospect and indirectly does this manager produce the impression of the spontaneous and organic.]

[27]Ibid., p. 185. [Lowe-Porter, p. 184: ...it was the music of the words themselves which led me to make the gift {an original edition of Brentano poems given to Leverkühn by Zeitblom}--music which lies in these verses, so lightly slumbering that the slightest touch of the gifted hand was enough to awake it.]

Die variative Durchführung breitet sich über die ganze Sonate [Beethoven's] aus. Sie tut das bei Brahms, als thematische Arbeit, noch durchgreifender und umfassender. Nimmt ihn als Beispiel dafür, <u>wie Subjektivität in Objektivität sich wandelt</u>! [emphasis mine] Bei ihm entäussert sich die Musik aller konventionellen Floskeln, Formeln und Rückstände und erzeugt sozusagen die Einheit des Werks jeden Augenblick neu, aus Freiheit. Aber gerade damit wird die Freiheit zum Prinzip allseitiger Ökonomie, das der Musik nichts Zufälliges lässt und noch die äusserste Mannigfaltigkeit aus identisch festgehaltenen Materialien entwickelt. Wo es nichts Unthematisches mehr gibt, nichts, was sich nicht als Ableitung eines immer Gleichen ausweisen könnte, da lässt sich kaum noch von freiem Satze sprechen....[28]

Leverkühn appears to have been a diligent student because the above passage is identical in many respects to Kretzschmar's analysis of Beethoven's Op. 111 and serves to strengthen the idea of a common musical evolution extending from Beethoven to Brahms to Leverkühn.

The third historical influence on Leverkühn's 12-tone method is the idea of the emancipation of the dissonance, that is, the breakdown of the tonal relativity between "active" and "passive" sonic structures. Leverkühn views this as an historical phenomenon already in evidence in some of Wagner's works and which necessarily leads to an expansion of the role of counterpoint in music, producing what he terms as an "Indifferenz von Harmonik und Melodik."[29]

Leverkühn, therefore, is seemingly compelled by these historical tendencies toward a musical style that favors the specificity of the word, the organic unity of the variations, and the determined structural definition of counterpoint. The highly idiosyncratic nature of his later compositions is

---

[28]Ibid., p. 191. [Lowe-Porter, pp. 190-91: The principle of development plus variation technique extends over the whole sonata [Beethoven's]. It does that in Brahms, as thematic working-out, even more radically take him as an example of <u>how subjectivity turns into objectivity</u>. [emphasis mine] In him music abstains from all conventional flourishes, formulas, and residua and so to speak creates the unity of the work anew at every moment out of freedom. But precisely on that account freedom becomes the principle of an all-round economy that leaves in music nothing casual, and develops the utmost diversity while adhering to the identical material. While there is nothing unthematic left, nothing which could not show itself to derive from the same basic material, there one can no longer speak of a 'free style.']
[29]Ibid., pp. 192-94. [Lowe-Porter, pp. 192-93.]

doubly ironic in that it is the result of an artistic style less the product of individual will than of an acutely prevalent historicism, and this artistic style becomes so deterministic as to negate the creative role of the composer.

After Adrian has conceptualized his new method of composition, he and Rüdiger Schildknapp travel to the town of Palestrina in Italy for a vacation. Leverkühn's room in the pensione becomes the venue of the remarkable "dialogue" with the Devil. Mann's choice of the birthplace of Giovanni Pierluigi da Palestrina, whose compositions represent the summa of the Counter-Reformation, is hardly accidental. Not only is there a great deal of ironical contrast in the biographical details and compositional methodologies of the two composers, but also in the linking of these two widely disparate individuals there is the reminder of the underlying premises of the novel, namely, that all music contains demonic propensities to one degree or another. Even in the pious nobility of Palestrina's masses and the controlled functioning of the composer's contrapuntal style there is that spark of creativity that is of demonic inspiration. The analogy between Leverkühn and Palestrina is less strained than might be imagined. Both composers developed musical styles that were easily susceptible to codification and found creative inspiration within the limited parameters established by arbitrary artistic rules. Palestrina's compositions represent a Mannian "breakthrough" of sorts in that they begin the harmonic evolution from church modality to modern tonality which will subsume J.S. Bach, Ludwig van Beethoven, Richard Wagner, and eventually Adrian Leverkühn in an historical process culminating in dodecaphony.

Although there has been much critical discussion concerning the nature of the Devil as seen in Chapter XXV--whether he is a figment of Leverkühn's diseased imagination, the Devil himself, or a transmogrification of Schildknapp--this is largely an irrelevant question.[30]

---

[30]See in particular E.M. Butler, The Fortunes of Faust (Cambridge: Cambridge University Press, 1952, pp. 323ff) and Patrick Carnegy, Faust as Musician: A Study of Thomas Mann's Novel "Doktor Faustus" (New York: New Directions Press, 1973, pp. 79ff).

The Devil offers no new insights into the events which have already occurred in the novel, and the "dialogue" between the Devil and Leverkühn provides merely an aperçus of the first 24 chapters. The Devil's remarks confirm the deterministic nature of Leverkühn's life and reveal the degree to which daimonic intercession has influenced that life. Concerning the composer's illnesses the Devil remarks to Leverkühn that the two doctors who attempted to treat Adrian's syphilis, one of whom died under mysterious circumstances while the other was arrested, were "...in deinem Interesse beseitigt."[31] Leverkühn's migraines (and by extension his intellectual curiosity) are not individual idiosyncrasies according to the Devil, but are directly inherited from his father. The Devil also posits the idea that Leverkühn's fate is a necessity for the fulfillment of a quasi-Manichean dialectic between good and evil: "Hast du vergessen, was du auf der Hohen Schul gelernt hast, dass Gott aus dem Bösen das Gute machen kann, und dass die Gelegenheit dazu ihm verkümmert werden darf?"[32]

Equally deterministic is the Devil's view of music history. In a discussion of Beethoven's Op. 111 the Devil emphasizes the loss of tonal meaning of the diminished 7th chord (which has been previously discussed by Kretzschmar in Chapter VIII and mentioned by Zeitblom on page 191) "...durch einen historischen Prozess, den niemand unkehrt."[33] This irreversibility of music history makes Adrian's dodecaphonic innovations inevitable and necessary. Concluding his remarks, the Devil makes it quite clear that Leverkühn's life has gone according to plan:

> Von früh an hatten wir ein Auge auf dich, auf deinen geschwinden, hoffärtigen Kopf, dein trefflich ingenium und memoriam. Da haben sie dich die Gotteswissenschaft

---

[31]Mann, p. 234. [Lowe-Porter, p. 234.]
[32]Ibid., p. 236. [Lowe-Porter, p. 235: "Have you forgotten what you learned in the schools, that God can bring good out of evil and that the occasion to it shall not be marred?"]
[33]Ibid., p. 240. [Lowe-Porter, p. 239: "...by a historical process which nobody reverses."]

studieren lassen, wie's dein Dünkel sich ausgeheckt, aber du
wolltest dich bald keinen Theologum mehr nennen, sondern
legtest die Heilige Geschrift unter die Bank und hieltest es
ganz hinfort mit den figuris, characteribus und
incantationibus der Musik, das gefiel uns nicht wenig.... So
richteten wirs dir mit Fleiss, dass du uns in die Arme liefst, will
sagen: meiner Kleinen, der Esmeralda....[34]

and:

Eine Gesamterkältung deines Lebens und deines
Verhältnisses zu den Menschen liegt in der Natur der Dinge,--
vielmehr sie liegt bereits in deiner Natur, wir auferlegen dir
beileibe nichts Neues, die Kleinen machen nichts Neues und
Fremdes aus dir, sie verstärken und übertreiben nur
sinnreich alles, was du bist. Ist etwa die Kälte bei dir nicht
vorgebildet, so gut wie das väterliche Hauptwee, aus dem die
Schmerzen der kleinen Seejungfrau werden sollen?[35]

As Adrian gains in stature as a composer, his circle of
acquaintances grows wider, many of whom function as manifestations of
his daimon. One of the most interesting collection of minor characters
fulfilling this role are the members of Sixtus Kridwiss' intellectual circle.
Kridwiss, an expert on East Asian art, and his confréres view historical
events with resignation and do not call for efforts against the "inevitability"
of historical processes. Although Mann ostensibly meant the members of
the Kridwiss circle to act as symbols of the acquiescence of the German
intelligentsia in the rise to power of the Nazis, they also serve to reinforce
Leverkühn's musical concepts from the perspectives of their own

---

[34]Ibid., p. 249. [Lowe-Porter, pp. 247-48: From early on we had an eye on you, on
your quick, arrogant head, your mighty ingenium and memoriam. They have made you
study theology, as your conceit devised it, but you would soon name yourself no lenger of
theologicans, but put the Good Book under the bench and from then on stick to the
figures, the characters, and incantations of music, which pleased us not a little.... Thus it
was our busily prepensed plan that you should run into our arms, that is, of my little one,
Esmeralda....]

[35]Ibid., p. 250. [Lowe-Porter, p. 249: A general chilling of your life and your relation to
men lies in the nature of things--rather it lies already in your nature; in faith we lay upon
you nothing new, the little ones make nothing new and strange out of you, they only
ingeniously strengthen and exaggerate all that you already are. The coldness in you is
perhaps not prefigured, as well as the paternal head paynes out of which the pangs of the
little seamaid are to come?]

disciplines. For example, Dr. Chaim Breisacher, an aesthetician interested in theories of decay in both art and religion, wishes religion to shed ritual and resume its original alliance with magic. This is very similar to Adrian's desire, as exemplified in his "magic square" tone-row matrix, to return music to the realm of magic via religion and mathematics. In addition, Egon Unruhe, a paleontologist, is a committed Darwinist, and Georg Vogler, a literary historian, conceives of literary history from a strictly racial standpoint. Both of these minor characters employ very deterministic modi operandi in their respective disciplines and contribute substantially to an intellectual environment in which Leverkühn's dodecaphony seems logical and quite normal.

Leverkühn's personal relationships display the same deterministic nature as his intellectual contacts, and the composer is fated to a life without the benefit of love. Indeed, all of the characters in the novel for whom Leverkühn has an especial fondness are disposed of in as mysterious a manner as the two doctors who attempted to treat the composer's syphilis. Rudolf Schwerdtfeger, the violinist for whom Leverkühn composes his Violin Concerto and who is the only person per du with Adrian besides Zeitblom, is gunned down by his former lover Inez Institoris, but not before Schwerdtfeger has an opportunity to play the role of Miles Standish in Leverkühn's ludicrous attempt to gain the hand of Marie Godeau. Schwerdtfeger, of course, is the daimon par excellence, a performer on the violin, the traditional instrument of the Devil, and an accomplished interpreter of Tartini's "Devil's Trill" Sonata. Most heartwrenching of all is the death by meningitis of Nepomuk "Echo" Schneidewein, Adrian's nephew and object of his uncle's most profound love. The deaths of both Schwerdtfeger and Echo seem to compel Adrian to the composition of his last and greatest masterpiece, Dr. Fausti Weheklag. Ironically, Leverkühn's position vis-à-vis love is no more than a hypostatization of the romantic ideal of the transfiguration of love through death. A very minor figure in the novel, the Hungarian musicologist Desiderus Fehér, is reported by Zeitblom to have remarked about Adrian's music that:

96

> ...[E]r sagte, von oben, aus einer Spräre, höher als alle
> Gelehrsamkeit, der Spräre der Liebe und des Glaubens, des
> Ewig-Weiblichen mit einem Wort, hatte darauf hingelenkt
> werden müssen.[36]

It is not, however, the transfiguring love of the Virgin or of a Gretchen (Marie Godeau is, in reality, an anti-Gretchen) that "lures Adrian to perfection," but the perfunctory encounter with the prostitute Esmeralda. Leverkühn's death and transfiguration is not a shared event but a self-sacrifice for the transcendence of his own ego and artistic will.

Just as Leverkühn is denied requited love so too is he hermetically sealed off from the world, the world being the everyday association with mankind seen as a necessary component of civilization. Set apart from society at his retreat in Pfeiffering, the "world" manages to present itself to Leverkühn generally in the guise of daimonic personages. Two characters contained in this category are Frau von Tolna and Saul Fitelberg.

Frau von Tolna, based on Nadezhda von Meck, the mysterious patron of Chaikovsky and Debussy, is Leverkühn's wealthy benefactor whose aid is instrumental in promoting the composer's career. But the motives of von Tolna are unclear; she lives the charmed life of the wealthy aesthete while the peasants in her village barely manage to live on a subsistence level. Mann transforms the platonic relationship between von Meck and Chaikovsky into a Mephistophelian relationship between von Tolna and Leverkühn. Frau von Tolna is Leverkühn's procuress instead of patron, and, like Goethe's Mephistopheles, provides her young charge with the requisite materials for his diabolical endeavors. Notice the sinister tenor of the following quotation, all the events of which are implied to have their origins in the behind-the-scenes machinations of Frau von Tolna (or, at least, another manifestation of Leverkühn's daimon):

> ...--wie sich den nachträglich erwies, dass jene
> altfranzösische Versübertragung der Paulus-Vision ihm aus
> der "Welt" zugekommen war. Energisch, wenn auch auf
> Umwegen und durch Mittelspersonen, war diese in seinen

---

[36]Ibid., p. 389. [Lowe-Porter, p. 390: He had, as he put it, needed to be guided from outside, from above, from a sphere higher than all learning, the sphere of love and faith, in a word the eternal feminine.]

Diensten tätig. Sie war es, die den geistreichen Artikel im
'Anbruch' hervorgerufen hatte,--allerdings dem einzigen Ort,
wo damals von Leverkühns Musik mit Bewunderung die
Rede sein konnte. Dass die 'Universal-Edition' sich des
werdenden Oratoriums versichert hatte, war ihrer
Einflüsterung zuzuschreiben. Im Jahre einundzwanzig stellte
sie dem Platner'schen Figurentheater aus der Verborgenheit,
ohne dass die Quelle der Zuwendung klar wurde, für die
kostbare und musikalisch vollkommene Inszenierung der
'Gesta' in Donaueschingen bedeutende Mittel zur
Verfügung.[37]

Another character representative of "the world" is the impresario
Saul Fitelberg who tries to persuade Leverkühn to tour and aggressively
promote his career. Leverkühn is naturally suspicious of the impresario's
ideas and elicits this response from Fitelberg:

In der Absicht, Sie zu ermutigen, ärgere ich Ihren Stolz und
arbeite sehenden Auges gegen mich selbst. Denn ich sage
mir natürlich, dass Ihresgleichen--aber ich sollte nicht von
Ihresgleichen sprechen, sondern nur von Ihnen,--dass Sie
also Ihre Existenz, Ihr destin als etwas zu Einmaliges
betrachten und es zu heilig halten, um es mit anderen
zusammen--zuwerfen. Sie wollen von den anderen destinées
nichts wissen, sondern nur von Ihrer eigenen, als etwas
einzigem--ich weiss, ich verstehe. Sie verabscheuen das
Herabsetzende aller Generalisierung, Einreihung,
Subsumierung. Sie bestehen auf der Unvergleichlichkeit des
persönlichen Falles. Sie huldigen einem personalistischen
Einsamkeitshochmut, der seine Notwendigkeit haben mag.[38]

---

[37]Ibid., pp. 393-94. [Lowe-Porter, p. 394: It turned out, for instance, that that old-
French metrical version of the vision of St. Paul had come to him from the "outer world."
The same outer world was constantly, if by round-about ways and through intermediaries,
active on his behalf. It was "the world" which instigated that stimulating article in the
Anbruch, certainly the only publication where enthusiasm for Leverkühn's music could get
a hearing. It was "the world" which saw to it that the "Universal Editions" had secured the
oratorio while it was still being written. In 1921, it put at the disposal of the Platner
marionette theatre, privately, so that the source of the gift was left vague, considerable
sums for the expensive and musically adequate production of the Gesta in
Donaueschingen.]

[38]Ibid., p. 404. [Lowe-Porter, pp. 404-5: With the idea of encouraging you I anger your
pride and work with my eyes open against my interests. For I tell myself, of course, that
people like you...you regard your existence, your destin as something unique and
consider it too sacred to lump it in with anyone else's. You do not want to hear about
other destinées, only about your own, as something quite unique--I know, I understand.
You abhor all generalizing, classifying, subsuming, as a derogation of your dignity. You

98

Fitelberg as <u>daimon</u> has performed his task well. Adrian rejects the pleading of this odd figure and stays at home, content to follow his fate to its conclusion and finding individuality in the objective adherence to deterministic artistic forms and historical processes.

The fate of Adrian Leverkühn is every bit as horrific as that of Germany under the Nazis. The composer who serves as the receptor of musical trends rather than their instigator (and without the divine intervention as envisioned by Hans Pfitzner in his opera <u>Palestrina</u>) is a doomed creature damned to inhabit an existential void as meaningless as Beckett's Ballyba and as terrifying as any landscape portrayed in the apocalyptic novels of the post-war era.

In Adrian Leverkühn's world all art, but especially music, has lost its normative function, its ability to give order to a chaotic universe. As the protagonist of the novel learns very late in his life, even the extremely structured formalism of dodecaphony cannot restore to music its former grace and rationality. All of this makes more apposite Kretzschmar's remark that music is "...eine Kundry, die nicht wolle, was sie tue, und weiche Arme der Lust um den Nacken des Toren schlinge."[39] The last scene presented of Leverkühn as a viable human being has him, like King Ludwig II of Bavaria and Hermann Hesse's Joseph Knecht, standing in a pond up to his neck in water, having at last completely succumbed to the inherent irrationality of music.

---

insist on the incomparableness of the personal case. You pay tribute to an arrogant personal uniqueness--maybe you have to do that.]

[39]Ibid., p. 64. [Lowe-Porter, p. 61: "...a Kundry, who wills not what she does and flings soft arms of lust round the neck of the fool."]

BIBLIOGRAPHY

Arndt, Karl J.R. "The Effect of America on Lenau's Life and Work." The Germanic Review 33 (1958): 125-42.

Auden, W.H. "Notes on Music and Opera" in The Dyer's Hand. New York, 1968: 465-74.

Bates, Paul A. Faust: Sources, Works, Criticism. New York: Harcourt, Brace & World, Inc., 1969.

Beaumont, Anthony. Busoni the Composer. Bloomington: Indiana University Press, 1985.

Berges, Ruth. "Lenau's Quest in America." The American-German Review 4 (1961-62): 14-17.

Bergson, Henri. Creative Evolution. Translated by Arthur Mitchell. New York: Random House, 1944.

Berlioz, Hector. Memoirs of Hector Berlioz from 1803 to 1865 comprising his travels in Germany, Italy, Russia, and England. Translated by Rachel Holmes and Eleanor Holmes. New York: Dover, 1960.

Blackmur, R.P. "Parody and Critique: Notes on Thomas Mann's Doctor Faustus." The Kenyon Review 12:1 (1950): 20-40.

Boeninger, H.R. "Zeitblom, Spiritual Descendant of Goethe's Wagner and Wagner's Beckmesser." German Life and Letters 13:1 (1959) 38-43.

Boito, Arrigo. Mefistofele. Piano reduction by Theodore T. Barker. Boston: Oliver Ditson, 1880.

Brown, Jane K. Goethe's Faust: The German Tragedy. Ithaca: Cornell University Press, 1986.

Busoni, Ferruccio. "A Sketch of a New Esthetic of Music" in Three Classics in the Aesthetic of Music. Translated by Th. Baker. New York: Dover, 1962.

Busoni, Ferruccio. Doktor Faust. Piano reduction by Egon Petri and Michael von Zadora. Wiesbaden: Breitkopf & Härtel, 1926.

Busoni, Ferruccio. Doktor Faust: Dichtung und Musik. Wiesbaden: Breitkopf & Härtel, 1925.

Busoni, Ferruccio. The Essence of Music and Other Papers. Translated by Raymond Ley. New York: Philosophical Library, 1957.

Busoni, Ferruccio. "On the Nature of Music: Towards an Understanding of Music in Relation to the Absolute." Music Review 17:4 (1956): 282-86. Translated by Ronald Stevenson.

Butler, E.M. The Fortunes of Faust. Cambridge: Cambridge University Press, 1952.

Carnegy, Patrick. Faust as Musician: A Study of Thomas Mann's Novel "Doktor Faustus". New York: New Directions Press, 1973.

Conrad, Peter. Romantic Opera and Literary Form. Berkeley: University of California Press, 1977.

Dent, Edward J. "Busoni's Doktor Faust." Music & Letters 7 (1926): 196-208.

Dent, Edward J. Ferruccio Busoni: A Biography. London: Eulenburg Books, 1974. [Reprint of the 1932 edition]

Eliade, Mircea. The Myth of the Eternal Return: or, Cosmos and History. Translated by Willard R. Trask. Princeton: Princeton University Press, 1954.

Gatti, Guido Maria. "The Stage Works of Ferruccio Busoni." Musical Quarterly 20 (1934): 267-77.

Goethe, Johann Wolfgang von. Faust. Weimar: Böhlau, 1877.

Goethe, Johann Wolfgang von. Faust. Translated by Walter Arndt. New York: W.W. Norton, 1976.

Goethe, Johann Wolfgang von. Werke. 2 Volumes. Salzburg: Verlag "Das Bergland-Buch," 1950.

Gounod, Charles. Autobiographical Reminiscences with Family Letters and Notes on Music. Translated by W. Hely Hutchinson. New York: Da Capo Press, 1970.

Gounod, Charles. Faust. New York: Edwin F. Kalmus.

Grim, William E. "'An End Without Any Return': Thomas Mann's Description of Beethoven's Op. 111" St. Andrews Review 30 (1986): 125-34.

Grim, William E. "'An End Without Any Return': Thomas Mann's Description of Beethoven's Op. 111" [Expanded version of previous work] Paper read at meeting of the German Studies Association in Albuquerque, New Mexico on September 27, 1986.

Gronicka, André von. "Thomas Mann's Doktor Faustus: Prolegomena to an Interpretation." The Germanic Review 23:3 (1948): 206-218.

Ikeda, Daisaku. "SGI Pres. Ikeda Interprets Faust in Terms of Buddhism." Soka Gakkai News 10:192 (February 1985): 8-15.

Jantz, Harold. "Patterns and Structures in Faust" in Johann Wolfgang von Goethe, Faust. New York: W.W. Norton, 1976.

Kelly, James William. The Faust Legend in Music. Detroit: Information Coordinators, Inc., 1976.

Kerman, Joseph. Opera as Drama. New York: Vintage Books, 1956.

Kimbell, David R.B. Verdi in the Age of Italian Romanticism. New York: Cambridge University Press, 1981.

Lenau, Nikolaus. Sämmtliche Werke. Leipzig: Philipp Reclam, 1883.

Mádl, Antal. "Lenau und die Romantik." Lenau-Forum 2:1-2 (1970): 40-54.

Mann, Thomas. Doctor Faustus. Translated by H.T. Lowe-Porter, New York: Vintage Books, 1948.

Mann, Thomas. Doktor Faustus: Das Leben des deutschen Tonsetzers Adrian Leverkühn erzählt von einem Freunde. Frankfurt a.M.: Fischer Bücherei, 1967.

Mason, Eudo C. Goethe's "Faust": Its Genesis and Purport. Berkeley: University of California Press, 1967.

Newman, Ernest. "Busoni and the Opera" in More Essays from the World of Music. New York: Coward-McCann, Inc., 1958.

Nietzsche, Friedrich. Beyond Good and Evil: Prelude to a Philosophy of the Future. Translated by Walter Kaufmann. New York: Vintage, 1956.

Nietzsche, Friedrich. Jenseits von Gut und Böse: Vorspiel einer Philosophie der Zukunft. Leipzig: C.G. Naumann, 1891.

Nietzsche, Friedrich. The Will to Power. Translated by Walter Kaufmann and R.J. Hollingdale. New York: Vintage, 1967.

No author. ["Review of Beethoven's Op. 111."] Allgemeine musikalische Zeitung 1 (1824): 99.

Norton, Richard. Tonality in Western Culture: A Critical and Historical Perspective. University Park: The Pennsylvania State University Press, 1984.

Pascal, Roy. "Four Fausts: From W.S. Gilbert to Ferruccio Busoni." German Life and Letters 10:4 (1956-57): 263-74.

Perenyi, Eleanor. Liszt: The Artist as Romantic Hero. Boston: Little, Brown and Co., 1974.

Pickard, P.M. "Thomas Mann's Dr. Faustus: A Psychological Approach." German Life and Letters 4:2 (1950): 90-100.

Popper, Karl. The Poverty of Historicism. Boston, 1957.

Reichert, Herbert W. "Goethe's Faust in Three Novels of Thomas Mann." The German Quarterly 22:4 (1949): 209-14.

Rolland, Romain. "Goethe's Interest in Music." Musical Quarterly 17:2 (1931): 157-94.

Rosen, Charles. The Classical Style: Haydn, Mozart, Beethoven. New York: W.W. Norton, 1972.

Rothman, Tony. "A 'What You See Is What You Beget' Theory." Discover 8:5 (May 1987): 90-99.

Schenk, H.G. The Mind of the European Romantics: An Essay in Cultural History. New York: Oxford University Press, 1966.

Schlegel, Friedrich. ["On Hamlet and Faust as Philosophical Tragedies"] in Johann Wolfgang von Goethe, Faust. New York: W.W. Norton, 1976.

Schmidt, Hugo. "Religious Issues and Images in Lenau's Works." The Germanic Review 39 (1964): 163-82.

Shaw, George Bernard. "Boito's Mefistofele," (The Star, 18 July, 1888) in How to Become a Musical Critic. New York: Da Capo Press, 1978.

Siegel, Carl. "Lenaus Faust und sein Verhältnis zur Philosphie." Kant-Studien 21 (1916): 66-92.

Smith, Patrick J. The Tenth Muse: A Historical Study of the Opera Libretto. New York: Schirmer Books, 1970.

Spaethling, Robert. Music and Mozart in the Life of Goethe. Columbia, South Carolina: Camden House, 1987. Volume 27 of Studies in German Literature, Linguistics, and Culture.

Spies, Johann. <u>Faustbuch</u> [1587] in Paul A. Bates, <u>Faust: Sources, Works, Criticism</u> (New York: Harcourt, Brace & World, Inc., 1969. Translated by P.F., Gentleman.

Stamm, Israel. "Lenau's <u>Faust</u>." <u>The Germanic Review</u> 25 (1951): 5-12.

Vardy, Agnes Huszar. <u>A Study in Austrian Romanticism: Hungarian Influences in Lenau's Poetry</u>. Buffalo, New York: Hungarian Cultural Foundation, 1974.

Weisstein, Ulrich. "Librettology: The Fine Art of Coping with a Chinese Twin." <u>Komparatistische Hefte</u> 5-6 (1982): 23-42.

INDEX

Studies in The History and Interpretation of Music

1. Hugo Meynell, **The Art of Handel's Operas**
2. Dale A. Jorgenson, **Moritz Hauptmann of Leipzig**
3. Nancy van Deusen, **The Harp and the Soul: Studies in Mediaeval Music**
4. James L. Taggart, **Franz Joseph Haydn's Keyboard Sonatas: An Untapped Gold Mine**
5. William E. Grim, **The Faust Legend in Music and Literature**
6. Richard R. La Croix (ed.), **Augustine on Music: An Interdisciplinary Collection of Essays**
7. Clifford Taylor, **Musical Idea and the Design Aesthetic in Contemporary Music: A Text for Discerning Appraisal of Musical Thought in Western Culture**